T0365688

HOOKED

Flynt Rock

authorHOUSE®

AuthorHouse™
1663 Liberty Drive
Bloomington, IN 47403
www.authorhouse.com
Phone: 1-800-839-8640

Published by AuthorHouse   12/29/2014

ISBN: 978-1-4969-6204-1 (sc)
ISBN: 978-1-4969-6203-4 (e)

Library of Congress Control Number: 2014922962

Because of the dynamic nature of the Internet, any web addresses or
links contained in this book may have changed since publication and
may no longer be valid. The views expressed in this work are solely those
of the author and do not necessarily reflect the views of the publisher,
and the publisher hereby disclaims any responsibility for them.

Prologue

Here's a quick list of what this book isn't about: overcoming drugs and alcohol, fishing, being a bad performer on stage, or anything having to do with hooks. This is about one man's journey across the world, experimenting with the dangerous side of sex—prostitution, one of the oldest and most-successful professions—and coming out clean. Because of its illegality and stigma within most societies, most people view prostitutes as haggard, disease-ridden crack whores trying to get a buck for their next high. Having firsthand experience with them, I can officially say that hookers are some of the most generous, understanding, and daring people in the world and provide a service to people that is unlike any other.

These are some of the general questions I get asked when I begin to tell my stories to people.

"What do you consider to be a prostitute?" I consider a prostitute to be a person, usually a woman, who has fallen on hard times and gone to the extreme to help get by. To me, they are not bad people, but they are mainly misunderstood because society looks down upon them. You have to give them credit for putting their lives and health on the line every day to help feed themselves and their families. How many people you know have gone to such great lengths?

"What is it like to be with a prostitute?" In all honesty, it's not much different from being with another woman. I can say that it is more exciting because you never know who she is going to turn out to be. She could be your typical working girl just trying to make a dollar to get by another day. She could be a drug addict looking for a way to help support her addiction to her drug of choice. Or she could even be a well-educated girl trying to help pay her way through college. No matter what her background story is, she and the other prostitutes are still real people.

"Why would you even sleep with a hooker?" I slept with all of these hookers because it was easy and straight to the point. They show up and sleep with you. Then they're right back out the door. It's like a night at the bar or club trying to pick up a girl—but with all of the hours of talking and flirting and money spent on drinks cut right out. Plus, it's guaranteed sex, and you never have to worry about seeing them again and having to deal with dates and such. What can I say? I'm a typical guy. I see my goal, and I go right to it without overanalyzing it.

"Aren't you afraid that you'll catch something?" Of course I was worried I might catch something, but it was a risk I was willing to take. (And I can say that I've never caught anything anyway.) I was young at the time, and all I had on my mind was sex. Seriously, what guy in his late teens and early twenties doesn't think about sex constantly? I just did it in an unhealthy manner. On the other side of the coin, anyone you sleep with could have just about anything, so why does it suddenly become a larger issue once money is involved? Here's a little food for thought the next time you are trying to pick up a woman from the bar. It's like playing a game of Russian roulette—except no one gets shot in the head and dies in the end.

"What if she turns out to be a cop?" It's another risk I tested while choosing to sleep with a prostitute. And trust me—I have watched the undercover stings that they play on TV, just hoping I wouldn't be the next person to end up on the show, being taken away in handcuffs for the whole world to see. I can admit that there are ways for finding out whether she is a cop, but I'm not going to reveal them, because I still believe in the working girl.

POPPING THE CHERRY

For as long as I could remember, women always fascinated me—how they can use so much emotion to describe anything they are feeling and how they can use their sexual appearances to get what they want. It's almost as if they have a controlling power that a man will never figure out. I can officially say that women will always be one of life's greatest mysteries to me. I'm sure that most men feel this way, trying to juggle in their minds what women really want.

The thought of being with a prostitute came me to when I was in middle school. Someone told me how you could pay for sex and get whatever you wanted. No one told me it was illegal until I was in high school. I couldn't help but wonder why they would suppress anything like this. It's not like you're buying drugs or hurting someone in any way. That was when I started to do more research and found out about the human trafficking business.

I'll tell you right now that human trafficking is bullshit. No one should ever be taken away from what she knew, drugged up, sold to random people, and forced to have sex with the people who bought her. It's bullshit, and it should never happen.

I used to joke with my friends and tell them that I was going to bring a prostitute to my high school prom, but I never got around to it. If I had a time machine, I would love to make that happen. As for my home life, it was kind of shitty. I lived in a two-bedroom house just outside of Chicago, Illinois, with ten people, and I never really felt like I had a life of my own. I knew I wanted to go on adventures as soon as I could. I can say now that I sure as shit got an adventure.

I left home when I was eighteen for a job that I acquired, and I moved from there to Chicago for a short training period for my job. Then I moved across the country to Oregon, specifically Portland. Portland wasn't anything special, but it did have a huge meth problem. Every now and then, if you were lucky, you could see someone walking down the street, high on meth while making an ass of himself or herself. Yeah, I guess Portland wasn't so bad.

My job let me meet people from all different walks of life. It was like a giant melting pot. For the rest of this book, I will change everyone's names to protect those who are innocent. I will also change the name of all the prostitutes I met along the way to protect their interests as well.

My job caused me to travel a lot as well. I spent almost a year in the Southeast, having the time of my life. I spent some time in California and Mexico, where my story begins. During the summer of 2010, my job took me to the city of Tijuana. It wasn't bad for being just a little perk my job gave me.

Don't let the title of this chapter confuse you. This is not the first time I had sex. It just happened to be the first time I had sex with a hooker. The first time I ever slept with a hooker, I hadn't planned on it happening. It wasn't like I woke up in the morning and decided I

Flynt Rock

wanted to go out hunting for a prostitute to fuck. I was nineteen at the time, and I was traveling around a lot due to my job. This trip I had to go on this time took me to Mexico, a place I dreamed of going to ever since I was a kid, and I fell in love with Mexico as soon as I got there—the beautiful women, the sunny blue skies, the beach surrounding you everywhere you go, and let's not forget the year-round warm weather. It truly is a paradise you'll never want to leave.

I had woken up that morning bright and early for work, just like any other day, and I counted down the hours until I was off work because I had the next few days to myself. I was making plans with my friend Muscles to go visit one of the local strip clubs in Mexico.

As the hours counted down, the day seemed to get longer and longer every second that passed by. At three in the afternoon, the workday was finally over, so we decided we would stop back by our room that we were staying in during our visit and get ready for what would turn out to be a memorable night out. Muscles and I headed out the door around six o'clock that night and decided that we would stop and get something to eat at one of the nearby Hawaiian BBQ restaurants. I can say that Hawaiian BBQ is some of the best food I have even eaten in my life. I could eat it every day if I had the chance.

After we left the restaurant, we decided it was time to start our night out the way we planned. Muscles looked up the best strip club that Mexico had to offer, and we called a cab, got in, and headed over. As the cab pulled up to the club, the glowing lights of red, blue, and green mesmerized us. We got out of the cab and walked our way to the front door.

As we approached the door, a bouncer, who could have clearly qualified for the world's strongest man competition, asked Muscles to see his driver's license. Muscles reached into his wallet and pulled out ID, and the bouncer took a long look at it to compare the picture to Muscles standing in front of him. After about two minutes of silence, the bouncer finally opened his mouth to tell us that we couldn't enter the strip club because we were under the age of twenty-one. Can you believe that it took a whole two minutes of silence and a waste of time to tell us that we were too young to enter the club?

Luckily, we had gotten dropped off in what I would now like to call the red-light district even though I did not know this at the time. With a few more strip clubs down the street, we decided we would try our luck. It was the same story at all of the other strip clubs. You had to be twenty-one to enter. That was until we came upon the only strip club in Mexico that was eighteen and older. Now that I'm old, I can say that it seemed awesome at the time. But now, going to a strip club that doesn't serve alcohol is the worst idea in the world.

We walked into the strip club, and I couldn't help but notice that the entire club was empty and we were the only ones there. I guess that was what we get for deciding to go to a strip club at eight o'clock. Since we had the whole club to ourselves, we decided to take seats center stage.

When we sat down, Muscles decided he wanted to put on his sunglasses while we were in the club. This event was very strange to me. If you've ever been in a strip club, you'll know that it's poorly lit to begin with. But for some reason, Muscles decided that he just needed to have them on.

As the girls started dancing, Muscles and I found ourselves lost in the movements and flexibility that the girls were showing off. One of the girls there had hair that grew all the way down to the back of her knees. I started to realize that sitting center stage wasn't as good as an idea as I thought once she started whipping her hair around. There's nothing like getting smacked in the face with stripper hair to make you pay attention to what's going on in front of you.

As the next hour passed, Muscles turned to me and told me that he wanted to get a brick of cocaine and party all night long. I had never done drugs, and I never drank at this point in my life because I thought both were just a waste of time and life. I went along with it anyway and told him that it sounded like a good idea and we were in the right place if that were what he was looking for.

I can say right now, if you're ever looking for anything, a strip club is the place to go. There's always that one stripper who has connections to just about everyone and anything you could ever imagine.

We started asking a few of the strippers if they could help us out by knowing we could get our hands on some cocaine. Most said no because they didn't trust us and we hadn't found that one yet. A new plan arose from Muscles. He told me that we should go to the convenience store down the street to get a bunch of energy drinks and get all crazy off them.

It sounded like a solid plan, and we left the strip club. We walked down the street and went into the store, only to make a beeline straight to the energy drinks. My idea was to only consume about two while Muscles walked up to the counter with five in his hands. We paid for the drinks and walked out of the store and into the parking lot. We cracked open our energy drinks and started chugging.

We slammed all of the caffeine right down and started heading back to the strip club. As we approached an alleyway, Muscles decided that he wanted to walk down it to see what was down it. We took this detour, and halfway down the alley, we read a sign, "Flower Spa." Muscles told me that he could really go for a massage after his long day of work, and I agreed a massage would feel really great after that day of work.

As we entered the building, I was not ready for what would happen next. We walked inside of what was once again a poorly lit building. At this time, I believed that we were about to get mugged. A short little Asian lady led us to two separate rooms.

At this point, Muscles and I were split up, and the Asian told me that it was $50. At first, I thought this was really odd considering the fact I was in Mexico. I didn't think that a massage would only cost me $50. It seemed way too cheap, but I wasn't going to argue.

I paid the $50, and the lady left. About five minutes later, another lady entered the room. This lady was Asian as well but a lot taller than the first one. She told me that it was $150. I got confused at this point because I thought I already paid the money for the massage. The lady then told me that it was $50 for the room and $150 for the woman.

I could officially say that I had never been to a massage place that charged for both the room and the woman until this day, and it hasn't happened ever again since. I started to realize that this wasn't the place I thought it was, and I told her that I was thinking about leaving.

Just as I started to walk to the door, she told me that my friend had already paid. Leave it to Muscles to not think about what he was doing and just going for it. The guy once spent over five hours in the sauna without the idea of dehydration ever crossing his mind.

I decided I would give in and pay the money anyway. After I handed over the money, she told me to take off all of my clothes while she did the same in return. I instantly realized that I walked into a whorehouse, but I figured I was in too deep now to just pack up and leave. After I had gotten all of my clothes off, she told me to lie on the bed, if you would call it that. This bed was more like someone screwed a piece of plywood onto a few two-by-fours and covered everything with a sheet. I would have been more comfortable sleeping on the floor the whole time.

I got on the bed, and the lady pulled a condom out of her purse. I couldn't feel better about this moment after I saw the condom. I thought about all of the things I could have caught, but hey, at least one of us in this room was looking out for us.

I can say that she had tons of talent because she managed to put on the condom with nothing but her mouth. The next forty-five minutes composed of the two of us switching every thought-of position in the known universe. After I had finally ejaculated, I rolled over and thought about just lying on the bed for the rest of the night. Unfortunately for me, they kick you out of the whorehouse once you are done.

So I stood up from the bed and put on my clothes. The lady I slept with didn't really say much of anything; however, she did have one of the most awkward smiles I had ever seen in my life. I walked out of the house, stood in the parking lot for about five minutes, and waited for Muscles to get done and walk out.

Sure enough, he came walking out with one of the biggest smiles of his life, and he was now holding a bottle of tanning oil. I asked Muscles why he had a bottle of tanning oil in his hands, and he proceeded to tell me that his hooker gave it to him because he was talking to her about how he wanted to get the perfect tan while he was in Mexico. Going to see a hooker and getting more than just sex, it sounded like a pretty good deal to me.

I asked Muscles what he wanted to do for the rest of the night, and his plan was to still get cocaine and party all night. We started walking back to the strip club because I just knew that one of them must know where Ray could get his hands on some cocaine. We walked back into the strip club, and the place was now packed from one end of the club to the other. We managed to find a few empty seats, but they were all the way in the back.

I told Muscles that our chances of getting noticed in the club now were slim to none. I couldn't be more wrong in my life. As soon as we both sat down, four of the girls came right over to us and started to strike up a conversation. We talked with the strippers for the next few minutes, and I overheard one of the strippers talking to Muscles about how she went to Burning Man earlier in the year.

Ding ding ding! I finally found a winner. I turned to her, and I asked her what else she had done with her life. It turned out she was actually visiting Mexico, and she decided she would work just to make some spending money on the side. I never knew this about strippers, but when they travel, some choose to work on their vacations, so the whole vacations pay for themselves this way.

I finally spit out the question and asked her if she knew where Muscles and I could find some cocaine. She started laughing and asked what made her the kind of girl that would know where cocaine might be. I proceeded to tell her that she gave it away once she started talking about Burning Man. If you don't know what Burning Man is, it's an annual festival that takes place out in the middle of the desert. Everyone who comes puts on live-action art displays. If you ever get a chance, I recommend you check it out.

The stripper told me that I had asked her at the wrong time. She said she used to do coke until a few weeks before she came out to Mexico. I turned to Muscles and told him that we had missed our only chance of ever getting any cocaine. Muscles decided that there was really no need to be out for the rest of the night because he was not about ready to spend the rest of his money on strippers, especially right after he just got laid.

We called it a night and left the strip club. We got outside and hailed a cab. As the cab headed back to our hotel room, I looked at the street signs to remember the names of where the two streets intersected.

The rest of my time in Mexico would conclude with me finishing up the job I was sent there for, but I also went back to the whorehouse there three more times. It was like I found true love. I couldn't get enough of it. I can officially say that I have never been to a whorehouse since I left Mexico.

THE TRIP

A few days after my return to the mainland, I already wanted to go back to Hawaii. I was living and working in Oregon at the time, and I can say it doesn't have the nicest weather in the world. Sometimes, I had a hard time telling the gray painted on the side of a skyscraper and the actual sky itself. It rained every day, and it just brought down the whole mood, so you'd have to find things to help entertain yourself to keep from getting depressed.

I will be honest. I was using dating websites as a way to meet women, but you can never really trust whom you are really talking to. After all, if I posted things on my profile about my sex life, do you think women would stop to say hi to me? Most of the people who use these websites are drug addicts looking for an easy way to get their hands on some money. Single moms are looking for a baby daddy, or they are underage, pretending to be older just to get with older men. I don't have a problem with any of these things, but why pretend to be someone on the Internet that you're not? I can tell you right now, if you're honest with me up-front, I'll be honest with you. It makes everything easier that way.

On day, I was looking around on one of these websites, and I was doing the whole thing of typing a message and then just copying and pasting it to every woman I thought looked good. After all, no one really reads the profiles. My introduction message usually says something like, "I think you look pretty cute, and it would be really nice to get to know you. Blah blah blah." It's just enough to make me sound like I am an interesting person.

One day, I happened to meet this lady online who had long blonde hair. She had a little bit of extra weight but nothing too bad. She had a great smile and some really awesome blue eyes. She said she was twenty-four. Once again, I had to ask if that were her real age because I was not going to be the next person to be on *To Catch a Predator*. She confirmed she was twenty-four. I also asked her what her real name was. It was just another one of those things I had to make sure of. She told me her name, but for now, we'll call her Blondie. So we got to talking. She told me some of her interests and what she did for a living.

After a few days of mailing each other, she decided she wanted to exchange phone numbers. I gave her mine, and within a minute, I already got a reply from her. I should have taken this as a sign that there was more to her then what she was telling me. We spent the next few hours texting back and forth because that's what all the rage is now, isn't it? Finally, she told me that she was free tonight and would love to go out and do something. I figured, *What could it hurt?* So I agreed that I would meet her later that night.

The next few hours went by, and I spent them getting ready and trying to figure out how much money I should take out for tonight. I decided that $200 would be good for the night, not that I was going to spend it all. But hey, you never know what might happen on a first date.

I would later find out that it was a good idea I took out as much money as I did. The time finally came, and she picked me up from my house. Just to let everyone in on a little secret, I'm not the biggest fan in the world of driving because I tend to lose focus and run red lights. But don't worry when I take out a lady on a date. I'm still a gentlemen. I pay for the whole thing.

When we decided that we would go see a movie, the closet theater was at the mall, so it was about a twenty-minute drive from where I lived. Little did I know that a twenty-minute drive would turn into a whole history of a woman's life.

Remember earlier when I told you about the kind of people who used these dating sites? Yeah, this girl turned out to be a heroin addict. Now would you really start talking to someone if he or she were up-front and told you that he or she did heroin? She told me about this the same way you usually inform someone that a loved one has passed away.

I got into her car, and she told me that she needed to be honest with me. At first, I thought she was going to tell me that she was a dude. I started freaking out on the inside, thinking I might be getting raped by a tranny tonight. So I pretended I was fine, and I asked her what she had to tell me.

She came straight out with me and told me she was high on heroin. So, wait. Let me get this right. I was thinking, *I let this girl drive, I got in her car, and she's high on heroin. I'm pretty sure I'm going to die.* I stayed in the car. *Well, I lived a good life, and I'm not about to jump out into traffic.* I will say that I was surprised she was a heroin addict by how good she looked, although I will admit that I have met quite a few drug users who actually didn't look that bad.

As we continued our drive to the movie theater, she started to point out certain places alongside the road. Like I said earlier, this would turn into a history lesson because every place she pointed to was a place where she had bought heroin at. So I jokingly told her that it was good that I knew this for when I wanted to take up heroin.

We eventually made it to the movies, and that drive seemed like the longest twenty minutes of my life as I prepared for death. The weird part about this theater was there was always teenage kids standing outside, doing some breakdancing stuff. It never really made since to me, but it sure looked cool.

I can't remember what movie we saw, but I know it was a horror movie. Another great piece of advice is that, if you ever go on a first date and want to get a girl close to you, make sure you see something scary because she'll jump right into your arms, and it's even better if the armrest folds up.

The movie ended, and we decided that we wanted to get something to eat. Besides, dinner and a movie always go hand in hand. It's been a classic since people started dating. I decided to go to a local mom-and-pop restaurant, a small hole in the wall place. You know one of those places where, if you weren't looking for it, you would most likely never know it was there.

I settled on ordering chili cheese fires, and she told me that she'd never had chili cheese fries. How do you live in America and never experience the glory of having hot chili and melted cheese just smothered over your fries? I made her try it, and after a while, it seemed like she was eating more off my plate then her own, but hey, that was fine with me because I'm not really big on leftovers anyway.

We got our bill. I paid because I'm a nice guy like that, and we started heading back to my place. I felt like it was time to be honest with her because she was honest with me. I told her that I'd had sex with prostitutes. She told me that it was okay. Really? That was apparently all it took, to tell someone you sleep with hookers and she was cool with it. Well, now I know the reason why she was so cool with it. She then told me she was going to offer me a blow job for money anyway, but now that I came out with it, she didn't feel so scared to ask.

At the time, I didn't think about asking her if she had AIDS or HIV. I just thought it was my lucky day. After all, it was the first date, except now she went from being another girl to a hooker. I asked her how much, and she told me eighty dollars. So I felt I had to ask her if the money were going to drugs, and she told me no.

In the back of my mind, I felt like she was lying to me, so I asked her again. And she said that, if I didn't want it, I could just say no. To this day, I still don't know if that money went to drugs or not. It most likely did. Like I said, I would later find out it was a good thing that I took out an excess amount of money when I did.

So I agreed to it, and all along the way back to my place, I started to wonder if it were even going to be any good because she was high. I asked her if she ever gave a guy head while she was high before, and she told me she did it all the time. Now I didn't know if I should take this as a good or bad thing. The good thing was that she probably had plenty of experience; the bad thing was that I could contract something.

We pulled up to my place, and we headed inside. Right there, she basically made a beeline straight to my bed as if she were in a hurry to get it over with. Ladies, if you ever want a guy to feel better about himself when it's only going to be a one-night stand, don't make it seem like you are in such a hurry to leave. Especially when you haven't even started yet, it really brings down the mood.

So as she climbed onto my bed, I headed to my top drawer in my dresser and grabbed one of my condoms. Come on, really. You didn't think I was going to let her put her mouth on my dick with her drug use and all of the other guys she'd done this with. I might as well just dig my own grave. I turned around and reached for my wallet to pull out the money. Once I got it out, she jumped right off my bed and snatched the money out of my hand. I was pretty sure this was a good indication that the money was going to drugs, but like I said, I could never confirm it.

She then stood to unzip my pants and pulled them down to my ankles. I sat on the edge of my bed as she got down on her knees. She started sucking my dick, and I could tell she'd done this before because she turned out to be really good at it. It was probably one of the best blow jobs of my life so far. She started off slow and got faster as she went along and started doing some crazy things with her tongue, like that one thing where people could roll their tongues.

About fifteen minutes passed by, and I was getting ready to explode now. She never told me to let her know if I were going to cum or not, so I figured she would be cool with it. That's right. I shot my load right in her mouth. It turned out that it wasn't what she wanted, and she instantly pulled her mouth right off my dick and spit all of my load right onto my floor.

Now I got pissed because she just ruined my carpet. I wasn't really big about my carpet, but I felt like I should have something to get mad about. She sat up and started yelling at me, asking why I didn't give her a heads-up. I told her I was just getting what I paid for, probably one of the best lines I have used to this day.

I then turned on her and asked why she spit her load on my floor. She said I was an asshole. I guess that's a good enough reason for me, but still if I'm paying for it, you shouldn't be able to be the one who's picky. She asked me if I had any mouthwash, and I told her it was by the sink in the bathroom. I couldn't help but laugh at what just happened.

She went to the bathroom, washed out her mouth, and came back into my room. I was still lying on my bed, laughing uncontrollably, and this upset her even more. She told me that, if she knew I was going to be this much of an asshole, she would have never agreed to meet me in the first place. I told her that she knew where the door was and she was free to leave at any time. She stormed out of my place, and I never saw her again from the day on. It was probably for the better anyway.

I did, however, call up one of my friends to tell him how my night went, and he couldn't stop laughing either. He instantly went on the same website and made a profile because he felt he needed to join in on the exciting adventures that these sites could lead to.

I haven't used a dating website in a long time, but I can say it was fun when I did. I do know of one time where a friend of mine did use one of these dating websites and actually got married to the woman he met online. It just goes to show that not everyone is on there for just a quick hookup.

THIS HAPPENED IN PHOENIX

I thought this would be a good name for this chapter because of the whole slogan that Phoenix came up with not too long ago. I had been to Phoenix several times before, mainly to visit my mom when she used to live out there. This time, it would turn out a little different, for I wasn't going out there to visit my mom. I was going to visit my cousin. I had also planned on going to the Adult Entertainment Expo as well, and it just happened to fall around the same time. I'll get into that more later.

He had been living in Phoenix for about three years, and I never got a chance to see him until now. I had just turned twenty a few months back, and it was that magical time of the year known as the holidays. I was leaving, and in a few short hours, my plane would touch down in the city of flashing lights and winners. I had stepped off my plane, took a smell of that fresh desert air, and made my way to baggage claim. If you've ever been to the airport in Phoenix, I swear you could make a vacation out of that place alone just by watching all of the unique people who travel to Vegas via Phoenix.

After I picked up my bag, I called my cousin and told him my plane landed. I got my stuff. I asked him where he wanted me to meet him, and this was the actual response that I got.

"I can't pick you up. My car's broke. You'll have to find your own ride."

Are you fucking shitting me? Trust me. This was not the first time he had pulled this shit on me. You would think, after not seeing him for three years, he wouldn't do something like this. So I took my bags with me and headed over to a bench in the middle of the airport. I kept trying to think of ways I could get out to his house. I looked around and saw a man in a black suit holding up a sign that read "Smith." Talk about a pretty generic name. Either someone was here with the last name Smith, or someone was here who wasn't supposed to be here.

The thought went through my head, thinking I should pretend to be this Mr. Smith until the actual Mr. Smith showed up. Damn, it seemed like such a good plan, too. I decided I should get a car even though I knew it was going to run up a bill I didn't want to pay.

I walked outside and hailed a cab. The cab pulled over, and the cabdriver was more than excited to help me into his cab. I started thinking that either this guy knew how to treat his customers or he was going to take me hostage and most likely kill me. Luckily for me, he never did try to kill me.

Now my cousin lived in an apartment complex that was gated in, so once we pulled up, I told the cabdriver just to drop me off and said I would have my cousin call the front desk to let me in. Something magical must have happened in that cab ride because now my cousin's car was running, and he told me that he was going to come and pick me up. So I turned around and paid my cabdriver. I took him for the ride as he drove away. I was left standing at the gate. My cousin's car pulled up a few minutes later, and he told me to get in.

We started heading back to his apartment, and he told me that his wife and kids flew back home to visit family. So for a majority of the time, it would just be us at the apartment. He parked his car. We got out, and we stood outside his apartment.

He showed me to the spare bedroom, and something didn't look right. I saw an air mattress with a bed frame. Now I hadn't even had my first drink of alcohol yet in my life, and not even when I was drunk had I seen anything like that.

I asked him why the air mattress had a bed frame. He told me that he used to have a bed, but he sold it a week ago. Really! He could have waited a few more weeks to sell the thing until after I left. Once again, these are the kind of things my cousin does to me. So far, this was turning out to be a great vacation. He then walked out of the room and went to bed because he had to work the next day. So I started unpacking my things, and as I lay down on the air mattress, I tried to figure out what exactly I wanted to do while I was here for the next two weeks.

The next day came, and I realized that the air mattress was a little deflated and it felt like I was sleeping on the floor. I discovered a hole in the air mattress. This vacation was getting better by the second. I picked myself up off the ground, and I did the same thing I did every morning. I took a piss. I walked out of the bathroom and found out that my cousin had already left for work.

I decided to look in his fridge for something to eat. After I opened the fridge, I found out that it was completely empty. I then decided to watch some TV, and I found out that his cable had been shut off. So I figured I would call him. He answered his phone, and I asked him about the fridge and the TV. He told me he didn't see the point in eating because it saved him money, and he stopped paying the cable bill over a year ago because it saved him money. Awesome!

It was a good thing I remembered to pack my laptop because I was going to need some sort of entertainment if I were going to make it through these two weeks. After my laptop started up, I looked to see if there were any nearby wireless connections I could get onto for the Internet.

Luckily for me, there was at least one that I could connect to. I still didn't know whose Internet I used, but I would just like to say thank you for letting me use it. If I didn't get to it, I was pretty sure I would have went insane. The next few days consisted of me spending most of my time on my laptop, watching viral porno videos and seeing my cousin coming home from work and going straight to sleep. That was until I asked him if he wanted me to just buy a plane ticket and go back to Oregon.

For some strange reason, this upset him, and he stormed off to his room and went to bed. I pondered for the next few hours if it were what I should really do, but I figured I was in Phoenix and I was still going to make the best of this trip.

So I went back onto the Internet and looked up local things to do in Phoenix. There were websites about the shows and casinos, but I was only twenty at the time. So it seemed like gambling was out of the question. I then looked up strip clubs in the area, and they all said you had to be twenty-one because they served alcohol.

Now, Oregon wasn't looking so bad. I then came across a site that was adverting prostitutes, and I started to think if I should really do it or not. I looked at the website a little more, and I started to like what I saw. They say that prostitution is legal in Vegas, and I could have made the trip. Yet I still got the same feelings as when it was illegal. I finally gave in and decided I would give them a call and just stay in Phoenix.

A few rings passed by, and they finally answered after the third. A classic in any book, you don't want to come off as desperate or uncaring about whom you might be talking to. A woman with a Spanish accent picked up. She asked me who was calling. I had never slept with a Latina before, so I instantly got excited. For some reason, I'd always wanted to sleep with a Spanish girl mainly because I have a thing for girls with big asses. I told her that I was calling in regards to the website. She asked me to be more specific. I wish I would I have thought about the next few words to come out of my mouth because it went like this.

"I want to fuck a girl. Preferably a woman with no penis would do exceptionally well."

She chuckled at my remark and told me that I wasted no time getting straight to the point. Well, why would I? I was young, bored, and horny. She asked me if there were anything specific I wanted in a girl. I told her that, with a voice like hers, I would take her.

Once again, she chuckled and asked me why. So I told her I wanted to sleep with a Hispanic girl, preferably one with a big ass. She laughed and told me that I called the right girl. She asked me where I was located, and I said about eight miles west of the Phoenix airport. She told me she'd be over in twenty minutes and I should have $200 ready, the most I'd paid so far.

After I got off the phone with her, I waited around for about ten minutes and started my walk to the front gate. As I walked to the gate, I started hoping that she'd let us fuck in her car. With the way my cousin was acting, the last thing I wanted was to give him another reason to act like an asshole to me.

Finally, I reached the gate, and I was early of course, so instead of standing around awkwardly, I decided I would talk to the gate guard. I let him do most of that talking because I kept myself busy by looking out for my ride. I'm pretty sure he told me his life story as if it really mattered to me, like most old people do. I'm sure you've had this happen to you when they'll tell you about life and what they have done with it. Even though times have changed over the years, they still feel as if everything still applies.

Finally after twenty minutes of being talked to death, in which time I would have rather been fucking my brains out, my hooker showed up. Now I had already had the money on me because I took out about $500 before I even left for my trip, so I just dug the $200 out of that. I walked over to her window as she rolled it down. Sure enough, she was perfect, a Hispanic women with nice tan skin, big juicy lips, and probably one of the best hip-to-ass ratios I'd ever seen.

When she realized that it was a gated community, she asked why I didn't tell her. I said that she didn't ask. So I told her we couldn't be here anyway, and I explained the whole situation to her. And to my surprise, she understood. I was expecting her to drive away.

She told me we could get a room, but I would have to pay for it. Honestly, getting my dick wet that night was better than sitting around my cousin's place doing nothing for another night, so I hopped into her car. Once again, it was another thing I should have thought about before I did it.

As we drove away, I only hoped that we didn't get pulled over. As we drove to the nearest hotel, we started talking and getting to know each other. She told me her name, but we'll call her Señorita. She told me that she was a Phoenix native and she had been doing this for five years. That meant I stuck my dick in five years or more worth of other guys' dicks, but of course at the time, I wasn't thinking about it.

I asked her if she wanted to do this with her life. She responded by sarcastically saying yes. She then told me she was a college student, but her family needed money so she started doing this on the side and ended up staying. She told me the whole story as we pulled up to the hotel. I told you that not all hookers are bad.

We were at the closest hotel, and in all honesty, from the looks of it, I might as well just had sex with her back at my cousin's house. It didn't have a chain name to it, and it didn't even have a sign. The only way she would have known this place was here was if she had been here before. Sure enough, those were the next words out of her mouth, "A lot of my clients meet me here." Okay, so now it clicked. Most of her clients must be cheating on their spouses because it left no trail with no sign or recognition with you. Now it all made sense.

We got out of the car and headed inside. The entire time, she was encouraging me to go through with it as she kept playing with my dick, a method used to make sure you're not a cop wearing a wire, but I was enjoying it too much to worry about that.

We got the room key, and of course, it was cheap, just like how the building looked. This place still had actual keys you had to use to open the door. We made our way to the room, and The entire way there because all she wanted to do was play with my dick. And no way was I going to explode before I got to the room.

We got to the door of our room, and I opened the door faster than the flash runs. I took one quick glance at the room, and it's just how you would picture it. The bed looked like it wanted to fall apart. There was the old TV from the eighties, and the carpet looked like a dog puked on it. I wasted no more time, so I took her to the bed and threw her on top.

I started taking off my clothes as she stood up from the bed and took off hers. After we both got naked, she asked if I brought a condom. I'll admit I always carry one because you never know when you might need it. I told her yes and tackled her onto the bed. I made her put on the condom. Ladies, it is a huge turn-on if you put the condom on a guy.

After the condom was on, I pushed her back down, spread her legs apart, and started fucking. This was the night when I found out my favorite position. I eventually put her legs on my shoulders, grabbed the bedpost, and started to power-fuck her for the rest of the time. A half hour goes by of me power-fucking, and she started telling me that it hurt. Another secret is that I masturbate about five times a day. Talk about a high sex drive.

I told her to shut up as I prepared to cum. Luckily for her, if I were drunk, that would have been a different story. I blew my load about three minutes later and fell over onto the other side of the bed exhausted. All I wanted to do was sleep because I drained myself of all the energy I had fucking her for the last half hour. She told me that we had to leave because she had other clients she needed to see tonight. We started getting on our clothes, and I asked her why she would still go through with having sex with other clients if she were already complaining about it hurting. She told me she needed to make money somehow. Talk about a hard worker. You have to give her credit for being a trouper and working through the pain.

We got on our clothes and stopped by the front desk to check out. I returned the key, and the clerk had the biggest smile on his face because he knew what had just happened. It wasn't like I really cared who knew. We got into her car, and for the entire ride back, we didn't say a word to each other. What are you really supposed to say to a hooker when it's over, something like, "Oh, that was great. We should do it again sometime." Let's face it. The chances of you seeing her again without calling her for sex are slim to none.

We finally arrived at the front gate, and I got out of the car. I stopped for a minute to tell her good luck in the future. She smiled and told me thank you. After that, I shut the door, and she drove away. I walked through the gate and made my way back to my cousin's place. I walked into his apartment, and just as I guessed, he was still sleeping. I went into my room and lay down on the air mattress, wondering what else my vacation might bring me.

I woke up the next morning, only to find myself in the same routine I was in right from day one. I kept trying to look for things to do, but sadly, if you're not twenty-one in Phoenix, there's really nothing to do. I tried to refrain myself from looking at anymore websites offering prostitution because I wanted to try to remember more than just having sex with hookers. That didn't last very long.

A few days after my first prostitute, I was back at it again, trying to find another one when I came across this one. She had a unique look to her. With her long hair dyed red, her face was made up of mostly metal piercings, and she had a skinny body that could even make supermodels jealous. We'll call her Metal Face. I thought, with a look like that, she must be a fun girl. So I decided to give her a call.

Once again, a few rings passed by, and then she finally answered. To my surprise, she could still talk with her mouth, even with all of the piercings practically holding it shut. She asked me who was calling. I told her I was calling because of the website, and she wasted no time saying she'd have sex with me for a hundred dollars. I liked how she didn't waste time, but to her knowledge, I could have been a cop. I made sure I asked every time if they were a cop after this.

I instantly agreed, and she asked where I lived. I told her eight miles west of the strip, and she said she'd be right over. So I once again grabbed the money, left my cousin's apartment, and headed for the front gate.

I chose to walk slower this time because the last thing I wanted was to talk to that gate guard again. It was good I did this because, by the time I got to the gate, she was waiting there for me in what I would like to call a piece of shit. This car was multicolored, and I was sure it was on its last legs. I got in the car, and I could instantly tell that she just wanted to get this over with because she didn't hesitate to drive away. I asked her where she planned on having sex at, and she told me right here in the car.

She drove to the nearest side street she could find. She pulled over, shut the car off, and said, "Let's get this over with. Do you have the money?"

I pulled the money out of my pocket, and she put it in her bra because she had no intention of taking off her shirt. She unzipped her pants and got them off quickly as I undid mine and pulled my dick out from my boxers. I took the condom out of my pocket. She climbed over to the passenger seat and started fucking me. I lost interest in this very quickly because I could tell that something was bothering her and she wasn't really into it. Ladies, a guy can tell when you're not into it, and trust me. It's a mood killer.

After fifteen minutes of her riding me, I finally told her to stop. Like she couldn't tell I wasn't enjoying it with the face of boredom I had on the entire time. She asked me if I came. I decided I would lie to her and say yes as I got off the condom as quick as I could to throw it out the window. I told her she was very young and asked her why she got into this.

Now here came the best part. She told me that she used to live in Phoenix with her parents until her dad got a job in some other state so they packed up and left. When she got to the other state, she realized that she left her entire life behind just to come back to Phoenix. The car we had sex in was the same car she lived in from day to day. I'll admit I felt bad for her. What was I supposed to do? So I would make one hell of an offer.

I told her that she should come live with me. I wish I would have asked myself what the fuck I was thinking. At the time, it seemed like a good idea. It would get one less hooker off the street and on the way to a better life, especially one as young as her, only twenty years old with her whole life ahead of her.

She asked me what made me say this. So I told her there had to be something better than living in her car. It was all she had, so I asked her again. She thought it was a great idea until I told her that I lived in Oregon. She said she'd never been there and didn't want to leave her hometown and everything she had ever known. I told her that it would be for the best.

It seemed like I finally had her until she asked if she would have her own room at my place in Oregon. I told her I rented a one-room apartment, but she was more than welcome to sleep on the couch until she got back on her feet.

She thought about it for a few minutes, but she came back by saying she needed her own room. I asked why this was so important. She told me she still wanted to work. So this girl wanted to move into my place and use my place to bring her clients and fuck then. I thought, *Yeah, that's really getting back on your feet. Sorry, lady, but*

I live in an apartment, not a brothel. I told her that she ruined that offer. After this, she tried to convince me that it would still be a good idea. I told her I'd see her later as I got out of the car. She wasted no time and drove away.

So now, I was on the side of the road. I was out a hundred dollars. I had shitty sex, and I offered a hooker to live in my house. Yeah, only I could pull that one off. Luckily, we didn't go too far from my cousin's apartment. It was a nice night out, so I made my way back on foot.

About a half hour went by, and I walked into my cousin's apartment. Once again, my cousin was sleeping. I only had a few more days left in Phoenix, and the big thing I was looking forward to was the expo, which would come and go.

Then it came my time to leave Phoenix. To end a perfect trip, my cousin couldn't even drive me to the airport. Needless to say, I still have yet to go back to Phoenix now that I'm over twenty-one, and I still have yet to have a Phoenix trip I actually enjoy.

THE ADULT WORLD

I figured I would add this part into the book to let everyone know how much interest I had in the adult world. The thing that first got my attention of the great world of porn stars was a poster. I was sixteen, and I was shopping around looking for things I could use to decorate my room. I came across this poster while shopping, and it was of the girl who had long black hair and tan skin lying on a bed with her ass popped up in the air. She was wearing a pink bra and panty set. I had no idea who this girl was on this poster, but I knew I wanted it.

I got back home and pinned the poster to my walls, along with a few others. I noticed that it had a name on it that said Tera Patrick. I still had no idea who this woman was, so I assumed she was just a supermodel. That was until one day when one of my friends came over to my house and asked who she was. So I decided to Google her and found out she was a porn star.

I wasted no time after this and starting looking up videos of her to see what she was about. I watched a few short clips from her movies, and I was instantly sucked into a world I would never leave.

To this day, Tera Patrick is still one of my favorite porn stars of all time. Not just because she is in porn, but she is also a successful businesswoman who has created her own company and overcame the odds even though life had gotten the best of her. To this day, I still have that poster with me.

I eventually would find myself doing more research, trying to find out everything I could about the adult entertainment industry. I would look up everything from porn stars to movies they were in to the companies they all worked for. It was nice to finally find something that was away from the mainstream media. After a while, the mainstream stuff is all you hear about, and it repeats itself because all of the original ideas are used up. The porn industry repeats itself, too; however, you expect it to.

As the years went by, I would still find myself getting deeper into it. That was until I turned eighteen and could legally go into a porn store. The first time I walked into a porn store, I entered the point of no return. I was like a kid in a candy store. I was in a world that I felt comfortable in. This was a world where everyone is at their most weakest. I say this because many people keep their sex lives private. At a porn store though, everyone can see what you are buying and what you are into. It's embarrassing for most people.

After I turned nineteen, I moved to Oregon, and I found one of the big chain stores out on the West Coast. I was a regular to this store chain only after a few months. It was getting to the point where I was becoming friends with the manager, the only woman I met who had a bigger porn collection than I did. I used to walk into her store and put my hands over my eyes, only to tell her to grab me whatever she wanted me to buy. I'll admit I had more money than I knew what to do with at the time, and about $200 of every paycheck went to porn or something else that was related to the adult entertainment industry.

After a few months of this, I was collecting more things than I knew what to do with. So I decided that I would help other people out as I turned one of the closets in my apartment into its very own porn store. I would loan the movies out to my coworkers. I had a giant box full of condoms that I would sell for a discount price, and I even had an industrial-sized bottle of lube that I would sell in small bottles. I would do just about anything I could to open up people about their sex lives. Besides, we all came into this world somehow.

This would all build up to me attending the Adult Entertainment Expo of 2011. If you have never been to one of these, I recommend you go. I didn't know what to expect when I first bought my ticket. Figuring that this was my first time at the expo, I bought a VIP ticket. After I got there, I realized I got more out of it than what I thought before. I got to meet some of the leading ladies of porn. I got to see the new releases of sex toys to come and get all of the free stuff that is handed out at the expo.

I did have a shirt stolen from me though. Some of the actresses at one of the big company stands were throwing out T-shirts. One was coming my way as I jumped up and grabbed it with my left hand. On the way down, just as soon as my feet touched the ground, the guy next to me ripped the shirt out of my hands as he ran away into the crowd. I lost him and my shirt.

I can say that this was the highlight of both my time spent in Phoenix and my time interested in the adult entertainment industry. As of currently to this day, I can say that I haven't bought any porn or sex toys. I feel that I had fun while it lasted and it will always be a part of my life. I know I'm welcome back at any time, but for now, it's time to focus on other things.

THE STRIPPER/BIKINI BARISTA/HOOKER

    I know what you are thinking. The title to this might be a little confusing, but don't worry. I'll explain it all as we go. Let me ask you a question first. Have you ever meet that one stripper that you just wanted to take home with you, but she was stubborn and only wanted to go home after she got done working? Well, if you have then, you can probably relate to this story. I can tell you right now that I never thought I would see her outside of the strip club, but I would soon be proven wrong.

This day started just like any other except we had gotten a new guy at work. Yes, we had our traditions to help break in the new guy. Usually, we would push them to their limits to see how much they could take until they got pissed off. It wasn't so much about how much they could take. It was more about the reaction of how they would react once they were taking past their breaking point. This was how we knew how well they would get along with us or not. If they were pretty relaxed and calm about the whole thing, they fit right in. If they reacted in a way where all they did was bitch and complain about how shitty everything was, they weren't accepted as much. This was because our job sucked.

So on this day, the new guy, AKA Old, had shown up for his first day at work. He stood about six-foot-one with a baldhead. He was in good shape and had a face that looked like it belonged in the movies. From his appearance, it looked like he was going to fit in with no problem, but we always had to make sure. The entire day was spent making him do meaningless jobs that really either had no end or no point to them at all. After a whole day of abuse, he asked us if every day were like that. So as our reply, we told him to get used to it because these kind of days were going to happen a lot.

After work, I approached Old and asked him if he had any plans for the night. Being the new guy, I could understand that it sucked, especially when you move to a new area you know almost nothing about. He told me that his night was to go home and sleep while he would get ready for another day of physical and mental abuse. I called him a bitch and told him to come out with me. After all, if he went home and went to bed, he would have been stuck in that routine forever. He asked me what I had in mind. I then asked him if he were married. He said not yet, but some girl from back home was apparently interested in getting married to him.

Here's the story behind their relationship. Old was a year ahead of this girl while they were in school. They dated for the first three years of his high school career. He was the high school football star, and she was the prom queen, a match made in heaven. That was until she decided to call it quits. They both had no problem moving on from each other. In fact one time, her friend even pepper-sprayed him right in the face. Talk about a good breakup.

So after a few years, he left home and came back. He had been home for a while when she called him unexpectedly and told him that she wanted to be with him. Trust me. He did not want to get back with her, but he finally gave in after all of the nagging and decided he would do it if it would get her to stop talking about it. It sounded like a dream marriage to me.

After he told me this story, I told him to forget about his future wife for the night and come out to have a good time. He finally agreed, considering the fact he just took a whole day of being messed with. And who knew what life would be like after he get married? We left work, and we each headed back home to relax for a minute and get ready for the night. Around eight o'clock we started out on our quest that would soon lead me onto an adventure I was not prepared for at all.

It was around the time of Halloween, and it seemed like the perfect night to go out. We drove all the way down to Seattle to visit one of the local strip clubs. Before we got there, Old asked me if they served alcohol at the strip club. Since I didn't know the answer, I called the club, only to find out that it was a statewide law in Oregon that the selling and distributing of alcohol in any strip club is illegal. It didn't bother me at the time that it was a state law because this was before I started drinking anyway.

Old got upset about his and told me that he was going to drive a little past the club to find the closest bar. Luckily for me, the closest bar was right next door to the strip club. Talk about a good deal: get hammered drunk at one place and walk right next door to see a pair of tits bounce.

We parked the car, and I headed right into the strip club. Old headed over to the bar and told me that he would meet me in a few minutes. I walked in to find a strip club that I would actually go to a lot during my time in Oregon. This place looked like you might have caught something just by sitting in the chairs, but hey, that was my kind of place. To give you a picture of it, you walk in and see a vending machine to your right. And straight in the back is a pool table you could challenge the strippers to. Most of the club was made up of the main seating area where the girls danced on stage, and in the back was the VIP area. This would be an area of the strip club I would visit a lot.

During my first time in this strip club, I instantly saw girls dressed up in the sexiest costumes I had ever seen in my life. I took a seat and began to enjoy the show. The first girl who approached me was the shot girl, telling me that it was a ten-dollar cover charge. I paid it, and as soon as she walked away, the first girl of the night walked up.

And yes, of course, she was fucked up on something. She sat down next to me and told me her name. She asked for mine, so I told her. She would eventually come to me several times throughout the night, tell me her name, and ask me for mine, so I would give her a different name every time.

After an hour, Old walked in and took a seat next to me while he had a good buzz going on. Instantly, he got lost in the girls dancing on stage, but he would never buy a private dance from any of them. This was when I noticed the girl who I would meet multiple times. They announced her name over the loudspeaker, calling her "Promise." What that promise might be, I'll never know. She has long black hair and a nice, tight, tanned body. She was wearing a fishnet costume, cat ears, and a tail as if she were supposed to be an updated version of Catwoman.

As I sat there and watched my cat lady grind up and down the pole, another girl approached me. This one wasn't so attractive, but I knew there was a side to her that I needed to find out. She looked more Native American, once again with long black hair. And she was dressed up like an angel. I don't know many strippers that can be considered angels, but what can I say? She really pulled it off.

She told me her name was "Cherish," a very common stripper name. We got to talking as we found out more about each other. Then she finally asked the question: Did I want a dance? I could only imagine how much it took for a stripper to ask. I assume it's almost like a man proposing to his girlfriend.

She led me into the back, also known as the VIP area, and all you could see were strippers grinding up against middle-aged men who look like they haven't gotten laid in years. She showed me to a seat in the middle of the room, and we got to talking again. She wanted to wait until the new song started to start dancing. As I looked to my left, I saw one of the funniest things ever. The song was maybe thirty seconds into it, and this guy exploded in his pants. He told the stripper that he was done, so she decided to check just to make sure. Sure enough, she grabbed his pants full of jizz. I'm not going to lie. I felt bad for both of them. No guy in the world wanted to have that happen to him, and she also just had to touch some random guy semen. I sure hoped she washed her hands after.

The next song started, and Cherish started grinding on top of me. She told me I was sure a nice customer about a minute into the song. I asked her what she meant exactly. She told me that, in Oregon, because they don't serve alcohol, the strippers could get fully nude, and you are allowed to touch them. So let me get this correct. I could go next door, get hammered drunk, and come over here and grope any set of tits I see. Talk about a good deal.

She told me about that side I just couldn't figure out. She told me she liked it rough. She enjoyed being spanked and choked. I must have been in stripper heaven right now. Just to make sure she was not lying, I grabbed her right by her throat, pulled her hair back, and started grinding the fuck out of her. After a few seconds, I let go, and I saw the reflection of the biggest smile in the mirror. Nope, she wasn't lying to me. The rest of the dance would go on and off like this with a couple of ass slaps here and there.

After the dance was over, she put her clothes back on, and I paid her. I walked back out to take my seat next to Old, and he asked me what I was laughing about. I told him the story about what just happened in the back. He didn't believe me until Cherish walked back up, looked me right in the eye, and told me to come back anytime to rough her up. Old was in shock and realized that we found either one of the best or worst strip clubs in the world.

We spent another hour of watching girls shake their asses on stage and having to reject girls asking for dances left and right, almost like homeless people begging for change. Around one o'clock in the morning we finally decided that it was time to head home. The entire ride back, I kept thinking of how awesome it was that I got to choke a stripper, pull her hair, and slap her ass. It was one of those nights where you have some much fun and go back home to lay in your bed and masturbate to the memories you just made with you and some random girl, enjoying a few minutes in heaven.

The week passed by, and Friday came back around. I jokily told Old while we were at work that he should go back to the strip club with me tonight and enjoy his last weekend as a free man. As I sat there laughing my ass off at the thought of him getting married, he agreed. I didn't even have to twist his arm to get that response. It almost makes you wonder if the poor guy even really wanted to get married. This time, going to the strip club would be different because another one of our coworkers overheard us. Let's call this guy "Dick" because of the way he lived his life. Let me explain.

Dick looks like he could have been a Holocaust survivor because he has absolutely no muscle or meat on his body. He has a bad case of acne and thinks that every woman in the world wants him. He is the kind of friend who doesn't know how to manage his money at all. In fact, this guy lived in the overdraft fund of his bank account. If he ever borrowed money from you, good luck ever seeing that money come back to you. He went through girlfriends faster than the hare outran the tortoise, mainly because he would get drunk and be a dick. Then he'd tell the girls that he wanted to get married and have a family already. Seriously, give a person some space.

This guy also drove an actual death trap for a living. We used to call his car the Red Dragon because it had a mind of its own. Whenever you made a left turn, the car would stall, and the brakes would lock. The right front tire shook. The whole car shook between the speeds of zero to sixty. Trust me. This guy earned this name.

So Dick asked us if he could join us to go to the strip club. Old and I both agreed, "What's the worst that could happen?" But we also told him that he had to drive, knowing that Old was going to get as drunk as he possibly could on his last weekend before getting married. Dick agreed mainly because he wanted to piss off a girl he was dating because he believed in making the girl he was dating jealous, as if it made her want to get married to him, knowing that some other girl found him attractive.

If he were a smart guy, he would understand that strippers are attracted to money, not him.

The rest of the workday went by, and we all agreed to go home, eat something, and get ready. Around nine o'clock that night we all finally decided that it was time to trek our way to the strip club. We kind of gave Dick the inside scoop of what this strip club was like, telling him that you could actually touch the strippers. So now the entire ride was spent by him telling us that his plan was to pick up a stripper by the end of the night. So I told him good luck with that.

We finally pulled up to the strip club, and Old made a beeline straight for the bar next door again as I rushed right into the strip club to look at the selection of girls who were performing tonight. Dick and I took our seats over to the left side of the stage. And guess who was there again? The one stripper who told me her name like twenty damn times. So I continued to give her fake names, hoping she'd catch on, but still she never did. Dick's jaw dropped to the floor, just like it did whenever he saw a girl who he thought was hot until he realized that he needed to get himself together before he scared away the girl.

About an hour into the strip club, Old came back over with a nice drunk buzz going on once again, and he finally decided that it was time for him to sit and watch some strippers dance. Then a young girl came on the stage, "Daisy," a very common stripper name once again. She was in her early twenties with long black hair that reached down to her lower back with a face that made her look like a virgin.

Dick instantly got locked on to her as he got lost in ever bend and twirl she did with her body, almost like a deer looking into a set of oncoming headlights. I leaned over and ask if he found a winner, and he didn't say anything at all. He did nod his head. Finally, Daisy's set was over, and Dick told me that she was the one going home with him tonight. Once again, I wished him good luck as he walked away.

I leaned over to Old and asked him how he was doing, and I could tell that he was going to miss having nights like this once he got married. His exact response was why I was drunk. "I see tits, and I'm not married. Life is good." True words spoken by a true man.

As I leaned back into my seat, out of the corner of my eye, I noticed a lady had already sat down into the seat to my right. I took one good look at her, and before she could get anything out of her mouth, I asked if her name were Promise. She responded with a yes and asked me how I knew that. I told her that I never forget a sexy catwoman, considering I have one tattooed on my left shoulder. She laughed and asked to see it. I showed her my tattoo, and she wasted no time asking me for a private dance. Without hesitation, I let her show me to the back without fully knowing what would happen next.

Once again back in the VIP area, this time I was led all the way to the back in the darkest part of the room, and she filled me in on how the dances worked. We waited for the next song as we sat and talked about how each other's day had been going so far. The next song started, and she started grinding on top of me. That was until I found out what she was all about.

As the second song started, my pants became undone. I knew exactly what her strategy was, to keep the guest paying for more, and yet it didn't bother me knowing that I would be spending more money. She pulled my dick out of my boxers and started stroking it up and down. The first week, I got to choke a stripper. Now I got a hand job. "I fucking love this place" is the only thought going through my mind.

That was until I saw Dick come walking into the back with Daisy. So I quickly asked Promise what she knew about Daisy, and she told me that she had been training Daisy since day one. Well, that was great. If she were anything like Promise was, this was going to make for one shitty night. I felt I had to get a few more dances just to keep an eye on Dick, and besides, I hadn't blown my load yet.

Five more songs passed by, and I was starting to wonder if Dick really had the money to cover for what he was being charged for. I fucking hate going to a strip club and having to play babysitter. Finally, I took my mind off his financial troubles long enough to focus on what Promise was doing, but unlike the guy from the week before, I refused to blow my load in my pants and quickly rolled to the side and shot my load onto the couch. Promise was now in a panic, hoping her boss didn't find out as we tried to clean it up with shitty cocktail napkins and hide it with pillows. Luckily, the room was dark so the chances of it even being noticed were slim to none.

I paid Promise, and she asked me if I would like to join her outside for a smoke. I told her I didn't smoke, but I wouldn't mind hanging out and getting some fresh air. So we headed out back, and she lit up her cigarette and started smoking in a hurry, knowing full well the longer she sat outside, the more money she was losing. We talked for the next few minutes about how often she did what she just did to me. She said that she only did it to the customers that she liked. Then she told me that she really liked the size of my dick. Now if she were serious about that, I'll never know.

Promise got done smoking and told me she had to head back inside and get back to work. As she walked in, Dick came right out with Daisy, and she didn't look happy. The conversation went a little something like this.

Dick: She broke me.

Me: What?

Dick: She broke me.

Me: Please tell me she broke your dick.

Dick: No, she broke my wallet.

Me: Are you fucking shitting me?

Daisy: He owes me forty dollars.

Me: That's it? You don't have forty dollars?

Dick: No, I'm flat broke

Daisy: I have to go back inside and back to work. I still want my fucking money.

Okay, I don't really know what kind of stripper would just leave an costumer outside that owes her money, but I could tell that she was obviously not smart.

Me: I'm not paying for this bullshit. You always fucking do this shit.

Dick: Well, I'm not paying either.

Me: Well, no shit! Because you have no fucking money to pay her with.

Dick: Okay, so what's the plan?

Me: Do you have your keys on you?

Dick: Yes, I do.

Me: That's our plan then.

So we ran right to his car and burned rubber right out of the parking lot, hauling ass right down the street. That was until I realized that we forgot Old at the club. That would make for a great story for his new wife. Sorry, you can't marry Old because he got drunk and got left at a strip club. We busted a U-turn right in the middle of the road and headed back, hoping the strippers wouldn't be waiting to kick our asses. A word of advice, strippers are the last people you want to owe money to.

On our way, we tried to call Old to tell him to get outside. After about four tries of calling him, he finally picked up. I told him to just get up and meet us outside and to run to the car. As we pulled up to the front, he practically dived right into the car, and we made another U-turn.

We told Old the story about why we were in a hurry to get away from the strip club, and sure enough, he gave Dick an earful, just like any normal person would. Finally, Old gave in and told Dick that he would give him money to go pay that stripper. Old established this as the only place he could go to get away from his wife if he ever got too pissed off at her. As far as I know, he never went back, so my guess is that his wife never pissed him off.

Old handed Dick the money, and sure enough, we made yet another U-turn. Once again, we pulled up to the strip club, and as Dick headed inside, I told him not to get fucking distracted. He walked in, and a few seconds later, he walked out and got in the car. I felt I had to ask him if he actually paid her or not. He said he did, but with the way that he lived, who knew if that were true or not?

We finally were on our way back home as I thought all night about Promise. Knowing I would most likely never see her again, I still talked about a girl who had a shit ton of confidence, knowing she could get fired at any second. You have to admire her plan, too. It was like she had the whole system figured out. I thought that would be the last time I saw her, but it only got better.

I stayed away from the strip club for a while after the move that Dick pulled, but I figured it would be for the best. Instead, I would get my kicks visiting one of the local bikini coffee stands around Oregon. If you haven't heard about these stands, they are quite interesting. The girls dress up in lingerie, bikinis, and just flat-out bras and panties just to work and serve coffee. I have to admit they sure have a way of attracting tourists. In fact, the first time I heard about this, I saw it on TV, and it was the only reason why I was excited about going to Oregon.

A few months passed by, and I decided to go get some coffee one night from one of our local bikini stands. It was my friend Juice Box and me. He got the name Juice Box because we went to Canada and he was underage to drink, so the waitress brought him an apple juice box. He was Puerto Rican with the greenest eyes you'd ever seen in your life. He was considered to be the life of the party because, after he got a few drinks in him, he would start busting out into random dance moves until he passed out.

On this day, I had discovered a new stand that had just opened, and I can officially say that I hit every single stand in the greater Seattle area. As we pulled up to the coffee stand, I noticed that this one had an extra feature added to it. They had built a stripper pole inside for the girls to display their moves and make extra tips.

As we pulled up to the window, the lady standing inside asked for my order, and I always got the same thing, a blended iced chai tea. She turned around to make my chai tea, and she kept standing close to the stripper pole. I kept thinking to myself that I had met her somewhere before.

I started asking Juice Box if the lady working looked familiar to him at all. Juice Box was a ladies' man. There wasn't a girl that he couldn't get. What can I say? He had something going for him, and it put it to use. After I had asked him, he told me that it was probably some girl he had fucked and not bothered to call back. I gave him the death stare as he was laughing his ass off about what he just said. So I asked him again, and he was unable to come up with an answer.

The window opened back up, and she handed me my chai tea. As I went to pay for it, I told her that I'd met her somewhere before but couldn't figure it out. She told me the same thing. That was when she asked if I had ever been to the strip club. Instantly, it clicked in my head, and I knew exactly who she was. It was Promise. What are the chances of running into your stripper working somewhere else?

I asked her why she was working at the coffee stand, and she told me that she gotten fired from the strip club. I didn't ask for any of the details, but I was sure I knew why she got fired.

After we got done with our little brief moment of catching up, she tried to get more money out of me. She told me that, for ten dollars, I could see her tits, and for twenty dollars, I could see everything. She didn't even work at the strip club anymore, and she was still up to her crazy ways. I paid her twenty dollars, and right in the middle of the stand, she got completely naked and started playing with herself. Both Juice Box and I had our eyes locked on her and started wondering how far she was going to take this. She was only naked for about three minutes before she put her clothes back on. The costumers behind started honking their horns at us because we had been sitting there for almost fifteen minutes.

I said good-bye to Promise, and Juice Box put the car in drive. We pulled away from the coffee stand.

The only thought that was going through my mind was, "What are the chances of seeing her again?" I thought it must have been a sign, and I told Juice Box that I should have gotten her number. I spent the rest of the day pissed off at myself for failing to get that. I swear I don't even think I slept that night.

The very next day after work, I had Juice Box drive me back up to the same coffee stand to see if she were working. As we pulled up to the window this time, I noticed her picture in the window with her name on it. For safety purposes, I'm going to keep her name at Promise. Sadly for me, she was not working on this day, but some other girl with an amazing tan, long black hair down to her ass, and a Mexican complexion was in the coffee stand.

I asked her where Promise was, and she told me that she had gotten fired the night before for forgetting to do something while she was closing. I got so pissed off that I told Juice Box to just drive away. How could I let a chance to get her number pass me by?

As Juice Box drove away, I wondered if I would ever see her again. Like I said earlier, I guess I got attracted to a stripper who I hardly knew. It actually happens to more guys than you could imagine, even though you know it's not good for you. I can say though I've always had a rock star fantasy in my head, thinking I would at least date one at some point in my life.

A few months had gone by, and I still never did give up hope. I just knew that, if I kept going back to the coffee stand, she would be there one day. I considered the fact they said she got fired and never took her picture out of the window. Every day when I would pull up to the stand, I would ask for the picture, but they would never give it to me, even after I offered to give them a tip of any amount they wanted. And I wasn't joking. All of this for one picture? I must be fucking crazy.

Finally one day, all of my hard work of going to the coffee stand paid off. I was in the car with Old this time, and we had left right after work to head up there. Sure enough, when I had pulled up to the coffee stand, Promise was standing in the window as if she knew I was coming up that day. As she looked into the car, she instantly remembered who I was and asked why I never came to see her. I explained to her that I was told she was fired, and she confirmed it. Apparently, she had exposed herself to a cop, and her boss had to let her go because of it.

After a few short minutes of catching up, I finally put in my order for my chai tea. She turned around to make it, and I told Old, "Today, I'm going to make sure I get both the picture in the window and her number."

She came back to the window with my chai tea and handed me the receipt. She then cut me the same deal: ten dollars for half and twenty dollars for full. So I made a counter deal with her and told her that I'd give her twenty if she included the picture with her number on the back. She agreed to it and took the picture out of the window, wrote her number on the back, and got completely naked as she handed the picture to me. Even Old got lost in the look of her body, and at this point, Old was married.

She put her clothes back on and said good-bye to me as she told me to text her later. If you are wondering, I still have that picture to this day. I had spent the rest of that day hanging out with Old and his wife, thinking about how she gave that picture and her number so easily. Even I thought it was too good to be true. I decided to head back home after Old had his two beers and wanted to go to bed for the night talk about being an old man.

Once I got home, I sent Promise a text just to let her know that it was my number. I never heard back from her that night so I assumed it was the wrong number she gave me. *That's just great*, I thought.

I had woken up the next morning, thinking about how much of a bitch she was for giving me the wrong number. So I had waited until after work, and I went back up there with Juice Box this time. Once again, she was working, and the first words out of my mouth were, "Why did you give me the wrong fucking number?"

She explained that she didn't and did get my text. She just didn't recognize the number, so she never replied. Then the next words out her mouth really started to make me wonder because she told me that she wasn't cheap. I knew it could only mean one thing. So later that day, I sent her a text and told her who it was and to save my number. She said she was busy at work and wouldn't be able to talk.

The next day, it was Dick's birthday, and the guy did do some shitty things, but hey, I still felt that we should celebrate it. So we all made plans to meet up at Swamp's house. Swamp grew up into the back swampy area of Louisiana with muscles on his eyeballs and professional drinking as his second occupation. He wasn't the kind of guy you wanted to fuck with. We finally got out of work, and as I was walking to my car, I got a text message from Promise. It went a little something like this:

Promise: How does $300 sound?

Me: Three hundred for what?

Promise: For sex.

Me: How about three hundred for sex and a blow job?

Promise: All right, deal. But you have to come to me?

Fuck, that just ruined all of the plans I made with everyone to celebrate Dick's birthday. So I rushed home and got in the shower as quick as I could. Halfway through my shower, I heard a loud pounding at my door. I knew it was Dick, so I was going to try to ignore it.

Once again, I heard another loud pounding on my door, so this time, I figured I would answer it. I got right out of the shower without even worrying about drying off and went right to the door completely naked.

As I threw open the door, both Dick and Taco were standing there. Taco was a Mexican kid who showed his Mexican pride through and through. He stood about five-foot-seven with a buzz cut and a bunch of religious tattoos. Once the door was fully open, they both got an amazing view of my dick shortly before they looked away and told me to put on clothes. So I quickly told them the story about Promise texting me. Dick actually got pissed off at me and wondered how I could blow him off after we made plans, like he had never done it before or worse.

So I closed the door, hopped back into the shower, and tried to figure out a way I could make them both work. I texted Promise back after I got out of the shower and asked her where she lived at. This was when it got good and everything fell into place. Luckily for me, she lived in the same apartment complex as Swamp. Seriously, what are the chances of that happening?

So I called back Dick and told him that the plans we made were still on and I would be leaving at some point to go have sex with Promise. He laughed as I got done telling him the story, and even he couldn't believe she lived in the same complex. So Dick and Taco came back by my place, and we took off on our way to Swamp's apartment.

On the way, we stopped by a grocery store to pick up a cake. I'm not very clear on the details of what happened, but I hit on the cashier, and the bag boy got pissed off at me. Management told me not to come back.

We got back into the car after the exciting trip to the store and the half hour or longer argument I got in with the bag boy and security. We finally made it to Swamp's house, and he already had a beer in his hand and was ready to party. We kept it kind of small, but a few more people showed up, such as Old and his wife, Juice Box, and even Muscles. About two hours of me being there, Promise called, telling me to come outside and meet her in the parking lot.

I made my exit as I told everyone I would be back. It wasn't like it was really a secret of where I was going or what I was going to be doing. They all knew. They just didn't care. I headed down the stairs and found her sitting in the first parking spot, waiting for me. I hopped in her car, and she started to head to her apartment. Then she told me the exciting news about how she shared an apartment with one of her girlfriends and we had to wait for her to leave. This was exciting because her roommate was leaving to go pick up her boyfriend who had just gotten out of jail that night. How do I get myself into these situations?

We continued to sit out in the parking lot outside of her apartment, waiting for a phone call or a text from her roommate, but it never came. So eventually, we both got to the point of not caring and decided to just do it all in the car. I handed over the money, and first came the blow job. She unzipped my pants and pulled out my dick. She asked me if I wanted to wear a condom.

I will be honest. I don't do the whole condom thing unless my dick is going in your vagina. So I told her no, and she started going to town on my dick. The only sad part about this is that she made me play lookout, which is never fun because you can almost never get fully into what you're doing.

She continued to keep giving me a blow job as I tried to do my best to care about who might be outside of the car. After a while, I gave up on the whole lookout thing and focused more on having my dick sucked. At one point, she stopped and lifted up her head to tell me she loved the size of my dick again. Whether she was still lying, I'll never know. After about a half hour went by, even I was getting tired. That's why you don't play lookout because it takes forever for you to cum.

Luckily for me, that's exactly what I did. I decided to be nice for once and let her know I was about to cum, and she gave me the thumbs-up. So what do I do? I blow my load right in her mouth again. What she did next, I'll never forget. She picked up her can of Red Bull and washed out her mouth with it. To this day, every time I see a can of Red Bull, I always think of her and that night.

After she opened the door and spit out her now–Red Bull and jizz concoction, she pulled out a condom and put it on me. Then she took off her pants and climbed right on top of me. We started going at it as she jumped up and down on my dick. I could tell she was in a hurry with how fast she was going, but hey, it didn't bother me any, so I went along with it. Halfway through, she shoved her tits right in my face and kept them throughout the rest of the time she was riding me. Nothing like having tits bouncing up and down on your face. It's a small part of the American dream.

I finally came about fifteen minutes after she shoved her tits in my face. Luckily, she didn't wash out her vagina with Red Bull when we were done this time. She got off me and hopped back into the driver's seat as I took off the condom and threw it out of the window and into the bushes. She put her pants back on as I put my dick back in mine and zipped them up. She then started the car, got on the phone with a friend of hers, and said she was on the way. Of course she already had other plans. That was why she was in a hurry.

We pulled up to Swamp's apartment, and before I got out of the car, I asked her if this were what she planned on doing with her life. She asked me what I was talking about, and I rephrased my question. I asked if she planned on growing up to be busted by the cops, only having to expose yourself and have sex with random guys for money.

She looked at me and said sarcastically, "Yeah, that was the whole life I had planned ever since I was a little girl."

I then asked her why she never looked into doing porn. I mean, come on. She had the sexual moves, body, and experience for it. I thought she would have done great. She then told me that she always thought about it and was going to look into it. I sure hope she is living a better life now, no matter what she's doing. She deserved better, and she knew it.

I opened the door and got out of the car. I said good-bye to Promise, and this would be the last time I would ever see her. Just when you get to know someone, you sleep with her, and then you never see her again. I guess that's just how life goes.

I shut the door to her car and watched her drive away. Then I made the climb up the stairs, back to Swamp's apartment. I walked back inside of Swamp's apartment, and the first thing out of his mouth was, "How was it?"

"The time of my life."

He then made fun of me for the rest of the night, saying, "You paid to have sex with a prostitute, and that was the time of your life."

What can I say? I'm a simple kind of guy. It doesn't take a lot to make me happy, but the memories will always be there. And yes, Promise, to this day, is still one hell of a memory to me.

THE HUG

I have confessed to my friend Sing every story you have read in this book. One night, it just kind of came out when both of us had gone to the bar together a few years later. He did forgive me for all of it, and he was actually more understanding than what I would expect any friend to be ever in this type of situation. However, there is one story I haven't confessed to him, and this would happen to be it. So Sing, if you happen to be reading this book, I'm sorry for what you are about to read, but it's the truth.

I had decided that it was time for me to take a vacation from work and come home, considering the fact I hadn't been home in over two whole years. Now, I'm originally from the suburbs of Detroit, which probably explains my attitude about not really giving a fuck. It was the springtime, which meant perfect weather, hot girls in bikinis, and good times with my friends back home.

I had spent most of my time away from home actually not even visiting my family because my friends were blowing up my phone like crazy because I was the person who was always down for whatever crazy idea we could think of that night. Most of my friends even ditched school and work just to hang out with me when they found out I was home for my short visit.

This day happened to be a little different. I actually woke up at my friend Sing's house. Sing had woken up early that day because he had to go to work, but he asked me if I wanted to go out to the bar with him that night to meet his new group of friends that he started hanging out with. I figured it would be a good idea to go. After all, it wasn't like I was doing much besides hanging out with all of my other friends anyway.

Sing is middle-aged and in good shape, and he's always finding new hobbies that he can learn to keep himself busy. For instance, he once decided to take up ghost hunting for a living, and he left for an entire weekend because he got addicted to ghost hunters and wanted to give it a try himself. Sing, once again, I'm sorry, but we used your house that weekend and threw a party. Another good example would be when he wanted to start making his own cartoon series. He locked himself in his office for about two weeks and made a whole series, but he never did anything with it. Trust me. He's always doing things like this.

Sing's new hobby happened to be karaoke. I have no idea why he chose this, but hey, to each his own. In all honesty, he's actually really good, and he usually gets everyone's attention. So he got together with a bunch of other karaoke fanatics, and these are the people he wanted me to meet. I agreed because I really had nothing else planned for that day.

Sure enough, as soon as I agreed to go and hang out with Dot for the night, my other friends started blowing up my phone, asking me if I wanted to hang out. Even after I explained the situation to them, they all agreed to just meet me at the bar and chill anyway. Talk about some badass friends.

After I had all of my friends agreeing to the plans that we all just made, I had slept the better part of the day away, mainly due to the fact I was used to a three-hour time difference. I woke up around two o'clock in the afternoon and finally got out of my bed and got ready for the day, even though I knew it would be hours until I even went to the bar. Sing had come home about an hour after I woke up, so he and I spent the next few hours catching up on how things had been between our lives.

A few hours had passed, and he asked me if I were still going with him to the bar. I told him the plan that my friends were going to meet us at the bar, and I would probably leave with them to go do whatever they had in mind for the night. Once again, Sing got excited because he knew he'd have a crowd at the bar to watch him do his karaoke thing. Yes, my other friends did stay around for a while to watch Sing perform, and even his talent blew them away.

Sing had to leave for a while because he said he had to take care of something. And he said he would swing back by the house after it was over and just take me to work with him and go to the bar from there. So instantly, ideas started clicking in my head, and sure enough, I started thinking about getting a hooker to come over. The only reason I wanted to do this was that both my cousin and my sister had sex in the same bed I slept in for years, and I figured I should join the club.

I watched Sing walk out the door and drive away. Instantly, I got on the computer to find any girls who were local and willing to make a call. I came across one girl, a short Hispanic with long black hair and a Brazilian butt. I'll be honest. I'm a sucker for a nice tan and a fat ass. I gave her a call, only to hear one of the best voices I'd ever heard in the world. It was like the right combination of Mexican American flowing out of her mouth as if both of the cultures were mixing together in my ears.

We had our short conversation on the phone as I asked her if she were the girl from the ad on the Internet, just to make sure I was talking to the same person. She confirmed and got my address to my house. She told me that it would take about ten to fifteen minutes before she could get out to my house. In my head, I did the calculations and thought it was enough time for her to come over, have sex with her, and get her out the door before Sing got back from work.

I hung up the phone with her and made sure that everything was ready. Sing had a cat at his house that he didn't take care of, and the cat did nothing but smell the house up, so I had to make sure the house was clean. I spent about a half hour cleaning before I realized she was past the time that she said she would arrive. I started to realize that my plans were falling apart in front of me. I thought the worse would be Sing catching me having sex with a hooker when he walked into his house, but that was the last thing I wanted to happen.

I tried to avoid all of this by calling back Sing and telling him not to worry about picking me up and just to come and get me after work. I thought all of this would work, but of course, leave it to Sing to need to come back and pick up something he purposely left behind anyway.

Once he told me that he would be coming back to the house, I started to panic and tried to figure out a different plan. I called her to find out how far she was away from my house, hoping she was nowhere close by. Sadly, she gave me the same answer and told me that she was ten to fifteen minutes away. Talk about not getting the answers you want.

After I hung up the phone with her, I tried to come up with a reason why I might have a hooker coming over. Not that I would tell Sing to his face who she was, but I still needed a backstory as to who she could have been. Finally, I thought of it and decided she would be a girl I went to school with who wanted to see me while I was home. Now I was only hoping that Sing would have already come and left by the time she showed up. Every second that passed by only made the feeling worse.

The next few minutes must have flown by because I turned around in the kitchen for a second, only to hear a car door slam. I rushed to the front door, but on my way there, I heard a second car door slam. At first, I didn't think anything of the second car door slamming because Sing usually had to get something out of his backseat. Sure enough, when I looked out the door, I was wrong.

Sing, if you're reading this book, I just want to let you know that this is the part that I'm sorry about. The sight I saw while I was looking out the door was my friend Sing hugging the hooker, but he only did this because he assumed that she was a friend of mine. Their conversation went something like this when they both got out of their cars.

Hooker: Oh, were you going somewhere?

Sing: Yeah, I have to go back to work.

Hooker: Am I late? Sorry I was stuck in traffic.

Sing: I don't think you're late for anything.

Hooker: So we still have time?

Sing: I guess we have time to meet each other for a few minutes, but I really have to go.

Hooker: Just a few minutes?

Sing: Yeah, aren't you here to see my friend?

Hooker (as it clicks in her head): Yes, I am!

Right after that, Sing decided to hug her and properly introduce himself to her. The only thought that was going through my mind was, "Holy shit! My friend just hugged a hooker." Not a lot of people can say that has happened in their lives. I will admit it is one of those times where, whenever I need a good laugh, I look back at that moment and think to myself, "Yeah, things like that happen in my life."

Sing walked her into the house to let me know that my friend showed up and he had to get some things for work and would be back later. She and I both took a seat on the couch as I apologized for Sing being home and said he wasn't supposed to be. She said it didn't bother her, but even she thought it was funny that I came up with a backstory and that my friend would have the balls to hug a random stranger.

We sat on the couch for about the next five minutes as Sing rummaged through his room and looked for whatever he thought he might need for work that night. Finally, he came out of his room and said good-bye to us as he left, reminding me once more that he would be back later.

Once we heard the front door slam, we dashed straight to my bedroom, wasting no more time. I showed her my bed, asking her if it would be big enough, considering the fact it was the same bed I'd had since I was a small child. I'm not going to lie. I outgrew that bed about ten years ago. She said it would be as I watched her take off her clothes. One thing good about hookers is that, if you keep your clothes on after they already get naked, they take yours off for you. So it's really like they do all of the work.

She got all of my clothes off, and she had me sit on the edge of my bed. Now the usual routine, if you haven't learned by now, is that the blow job always comes first, whether it is to get you off or warm you up. Either way, it feels amazing. She chose to do the warm-up routine, and then she had me get on my bed. Now comes from the other part of the routine. It starts out in the missionary position for a few minutes and then moves into doggie style. This is usually how it goes because, for most men in America, doggie style happens to be their favorite position, and it usually gets most of them off.

We went through with the routine of sexual positions, but for me, it usually ended with me on top and her knees by her head, like it did this time. After that, I rolled over in bed, and we both took a minute to catch our breath. She looked at me and asked me how I liked it. So I told her that she wasn't the first woman I've paid to have sex with, but I told her I wouldn't forget about her either. Little did I know that I wouldn't forget about her—not because of the sex but because of something she said to me.

After I got done talking to her, she got up off my bed and put her clothes back on. So I did the same. I walked her to my front door and opened it for her. The next words I heard stuck with me for a long time.

"The young ones are always the assholes."

At first, I didn't understand what she meant. I asked her to explain, and she told me that, compared to her older clients she had, I was considered an asshole. I mean, I get it that most guys in their twenties only have one thing on their minds, to have as much sex as they can, but she was a prostitute. So what separated me from them?

Once I asked this question, she let it all come out. She told me that most of her older clients buy her flowers and take her out on a nice date before they get down to the sex part. They usually give her a big tip and offer to buy her almost anything in the world. To me, it sounded more like a sugar daddy. Shortly after that, she asked me if it felt good watching her walk out the door after what just happened. I knew what she was trying to do. She was trying to make me grow up. At the time, I couldn't say that it worked, but nowadays, it has changed a little.

As I stood there in the doorway, I watched her get into her car and pull out of my driveway to only to drive away and become a image in the distance. I can officially say that one woman who I barely knew has made me think so hard about what I was doing with my life, but she seemed to get to the point. I can say I didn't let this stop me at this time. Come on. You didn't think that one person's words were going to stop me dead in my tracks, did you?

This was the only time I ever brought a prostitute into Sing's house, and I can officially say that I don't plan on having it happen again. The bed that everyone had sex in was finally taken out of Sing's house, along with all of its dirty memories.

The lesson I've learned out of this story is that, no matter what a person might do for a living or no matter whom he or she is, he or she has a better understanding of life than what you might think. This is where my saying came in. "Hookers are nice people, smart people, but not like normal people."

I REMEMBER MY FIRST DRINK

I seriously do remember my first drink and how it went down. This story has nothing to do with any prostitutes, but I felt I should add it because, up until this point, I hated drinking and drugs. I wouldn't even smoke a cigarette because I thought it was a waste of time and money. Seriously, who wanted to spend money on something that was going to make them black out or give them health problems, only to wake up the next day and feel like shit all over? That was how I thought until this day.

I was still at home, and a few days had passed. My friends were still calling me, trying to get me to hang out with them every second of the day. I had yet to visit my mom. It's not so much that I don't like my mom. It's the fact that everyone is in pain over at her house. By that, I mean everyone is broke and crippled in some way, and all they do is bitch about how much his or her body hurts and all of the pills he or she has to take. I swear that it's like walking into a senior citizen home.

I didn't tell my mom I had come home for a visit because my phone would have been blowing up, asking me to come over. The downside to this is that, if I didn't come over after all of those phone calls, she would have never let me forget it. So I felt that, when I came home this time, I would surprise her and just show up. It was my second-to-last day at home, and I thought it would be the best day to visit my mom. I did my normal routine of checking my phone for any missed calls, text messages, and new emails. Besides, you never know what happens during the time you're sleeping anyway.

A few days earlier, I sent a message to a girl I went to middle school with that I hadn't seen or talked to in over eight years. I told her that I was home visiting for a few days and we should hang out. I'm not quite sure what made her actually respond to my message, but she gave me her number and told me to call her. You would think that, after eight years of not talking or seeing each other, you would have probably forgotten about a person already.

We met back in seventh grade. It started out just like any other day. I went to school, sat in my desk, and pretended to pay attention until it was time for me to leave school at the end of the day. Within the first hour of being at school, that all changed very quickly. I sat in the back of the class, diagonally opposite from where the door to the classroom was. I watched as the guidance counselor was walking around a new student, showing her where her classes and locker would be for the rest of the time she spent here. I didn't get a good look at the student at first. As far I was concerned, I could have cared less really who she was.

I focused back on what the teacher was saying, only to see the guidance counselor approach the door again to tell the student that this was her first-hour class. As everyone looked in excitement to see who the new student might be, I was too focused on why the clock wasn't moving fast enough. That was until she stepped out from behind the wall and into the doorway. She had long blonde hair, an amazing smile, a perfect face shape, and a petite body frame. It sounds like I described every single model that you can find in any magazine or walking the sunny streets in California. Something was different about her.

She had her hair up in a ponytail, and she was wearing a gray hoodie. The thing that set her apart was the fact that she was wearing a pair of old school, classic black-and-white Converse and a pair of pants with straps hanging off them. She came off as the punk rock girl of my dreams. That was the day my heart sank. I wanted to know everything about her. Hell, I wanted to spend the rest of my life with her even though I barely knew who she was.

I watched as she walked into the middle of the classroom, and she gave her speech about who she was and what she liked to do. She said that her name was Love and she loved soccer, music, and running.

Then I listened as she laughed in nervousness because she didn't know what to say next. It was probably the cutest laugh I'd heard in my entire life. She took her seat in the middle of the room, nowhere near me. The clock hit the hour, and class was over. Everyone got up out of his or her seats and rushed for the door, hopefully having enough time to hang out with friends in the hallway before the next class started.

I instantly ran up to one of my friends to let him know about the new girl who just got to school. I told him I'd never met anyone else quite like her. I spent the rest of that day trying to get to know her as much as I could. We had several classes together, and I spent every break in between classes talking to her by her locker, only because it was right next to mine.

The rest of our seventh-grade year went by, and we spent most of the year not really paying attention to what the teachers had to say to us, only becoming closer and closer. Summer break came around, and I didn't talk to her at all during the break, but she was the only reason why I was looking forward to going back to school that year. The summer had flown by as I spent it between my mom and my dad's house, just like every summer before.

I woke up to the first day of school, knowing it was going to be a quick day of nothing but listening to the teacher talk about the rules and regulations of the classroom. I never did find the first day of school to be important. I always thought it was a waste of time. The only reason why it was worth going this time was because I got to see her again.

We had several classes together this year, and we had run into each other in the hallway, just like the year before, as we spent most of our time talking about what we did over break. The first semester of the year went by, and the second semester was just starting. Everything was going great until it all changed one day.

I was walking to my third-hour class, and the school security guard was escorting Love. I didn't think of it at first. I just assumed she was sick and needed someone to carry her stuff to the office for her. At least that was what I thought for the time being. The next day came, and she still wasn't at school, so I assumed she was still sick. Then the weekend came, and the next week of school started. There was still no sign of her, so I thought she must have had the flu or some other serious illness.

It wasn't until two weeks went by where I had to face reality and realize she was never coming back. The part that sucked the most was that I never even got a good-bye. It was a shot in the heart. I finally found someone that I was in love with, and just like that, she was gone.

Now back to the future, eight years later. She sent me her number and told me to call her later to see what my plans were for the night. I followed through, and the phone rang once. Then it rang again. As I waited in excitement to hear her voice again, my mind started to go blank as I struggled to think of what I should say. Come on. I hadn't seen her in eight years. What was I supposed to do? Act like I saw her just yesterday?

Finally, she answered the phone, and she still had the same amazing voice that she did eight years ago. It was almost like nothing changed. She asked me what I was doing tonight. I told her I had to visit my mom for a little bit, but after that, I should be free. We agreed to make plans, and then the next words out of her mouth were, "Yeah, we can have a few drinks tonight."

It wasn't exactly what I had in mind, but what was I supposed to say to her? I figured that, if I told her I didn't drink, I would have blown my chances of ever seeing her again. So I went with it and told her that it sounded good.

I got off the phone with her and got ready as I waited for my dad to get back from work so I could tell him I was going to visit my mom. My parents never really talked much since they got divorced. I can't say exactly why they don't talk much, but hey, whatever helps them sleep at night, I guess.

My dad came home after work, and I told him that was what I was going to do. He asked me if I were sure that I wanted to do it. I told him I didn't have a choice if I came home, and if I didn't visit my mom, she would never let me live it down. He dropped off his stuff, and we got into his car as he gave me a lift over to my mom's house.

During our drive over, my dad was telling me about how his workday was and the crazy things that had happened within the day so far. He asked me if I planned to stay the night at my mom's house, and I told him I had plans to hang out with an old friend of mine from school. This time though, it really was an old friend from school and not a prostitute. He asked who my friend was, and I told him that it was a girl I used to know back in middle school and I hadn't seen her in over eight years. He then asked what time I would be back. I told him I was trying to get back no later than ten o'clock at night, considering the fact I had to pack all of my stuff the next day.

The car pulled up, and I had reached my destination. I told my dad I would see him later, and as I got out of the car, my mom was sitting on the front porch, smoking a cigarette. I shut the door to the car behind me, and my mom was in a surprised state, trying to figure out if it were really me walking up to her front door. Sure enough, she asked why I didn't call her and let her know that I was coming home. I didn't call because

I've never really been one for all of the emotional thing. That is, whenever I came home or had to leave, my mom would always cry in front of me. I mean, I understand the fact that she's my mom, and I know she cares and worries about me when I'm not home, but I can say that the hardest thing I ever had to do was watch my mom cry. I told my mom I wanted to surprise her, and believe me, she was surprised.

I walked into her house to see all of my stepfamily, and sure enough, my cousin was sitting at the kitchen table. They all looked like they were in their depressed state, and that was when all of the talk about the doctors, the pain, and all of the pills everyone was on started. So I started to tune them all out. I stayed for dinner and played a few games of cards with my mom. I told my mom I wouldn't be staying long because I had plans to hang out with one of my friends. My mom had learned to expect this by now because that was all I really did when I came home for a visit.

She asked me which one of my friends it was this time. I told her it was a girl that she never met before, and instantly, everyone in my mom's house was all ears. For some strange reason, they all acted like it was some juicy gossip they all had to hear about.

I stayed for a few more hours, and it was about nine o'clock at night when Love called to find out where I was. Luckily, I was right around the corner from her house, so it took her no time at all to find her way over. Love pulled up outside, and I gave my mom a hug good-bye and said it was nice to see her again. I left my mom's house and hopped into Love's car for a night that would change my life. Love asked me how my day went and asked if I were ready to get my drink on. I finally decided that I would come clean and tell her that I'd never drank before. She refused to believe me and laughed as if I were joking. So I told her again, and she still didn't believe me.

As she continued to laugh at what I just told her, she pulled up outside the liquor store. We were both twenty at the time, so neither one of us could buy alcohol legally. Luckily for the both of us, she took us to the same liquor store she always went to because the guy behind the counter was too lazy to ID her. She asked what I wanted to drink, and I told her it really didn't matter to me. Besides, I never drank before so I didn't even know of anything that was good to drink. Love then told me that she would take care of it.

Love got out of the car and walked into the party store, only to come out about five minutes later with a fifth of vodka and a bottle of cranberry juice. I can tell you that I haven't touched vodka much since that night. I've become more of a beer, rum, and whiskey guy. She got back into her car and asked where we should go drink. I suggested we could always go back to my dad's house, knowing he wouldn't be there. She agreed, and we started our drive back home.

Over the entire drive back to my dad's house, we caught up on what happened during the years that we didn't talk or see each other. I told her that I had graduated high school early, I joined the navy, and yes, I even brought up the fact that I had slept with prostitutes to her. Even that didn't seem to bother her. Once again, I felt like I was falling in love. She told me that she got kicked out of our school district because she threatened to kill another student. That would explain why I saw her get escorted down the hallway by the security guard that one day. After that day, it seemed to be a lot different from mine.

She got sent to a different school district, and she ended up dating some guy she felt she was truly in love with. They had a kid together, and she had to drop out of school so she could raise her daughter. She worked a number of odd jobs, doing the best she could to support her and her daughter. The boyfriend ended up leaving her and hadn't had much to do with her or her daughter since. Still after her whole story, I found myself to be in love with her as much as the day I met her.

We pulled up to my dad's house, and I noticed that the lights were on, but my dad's car wasn't in the driveway. Now my dad had a friend of his staying at his hose because she was evicted from her apartment. She had a very unique personality, and she was from South Korea. Now when I say unique, I mean this lady would go out to the front yard and wash her hair in the middle of the day. She would throw bottles of water at my dad and me, telling us to drink more water, but the strangest thing she did was bake a bunch of sweets and put them in bowls, only to take them outside and hide them under the tree. I'm not quite sure how her thought process worked, but I could tell you that this lady was insane.

We got out of the car, and sure enough, once I opened the door, the Asian lady was standing in the front room, asking me where I was and flooding me with every question she could think of. I did my best to avoid her and get Love and me straight to my room. But I forgot that my dad's house didn't have ice. So we dropped off the vodka and cranberry juice in my room and made a second trip past the Asian lady. We walked out the door and made our trip up to the gas station. Sounds like a romantic evening, doesn't it?

Once we got to the gas station, we grabbed the bag of ice, paid for it, and got back to my house as fast as we could. We even tried to get past the Asian lady as quick as we could, hoping that she wouldn't drag us into another conversation. I was sure wrong about that part. Even once we got back into my room, she stood right there in my doorway, just to talk to us about nothing, telling me to drink more water and less alcohol. Little did the Asian lady know. This was my first time drinking, so she really had nothing to complain about.

Finally, the Asian lady went away after about a half hour of talking us to death. That was about the time when Love pulled out the bottle of vodka and filled our cups. She handed me my cup and cheered me. Then I took the glass, put it to my lips, and took down my first drink as I felt the alcohol burn all the way down my throat. After that, we got back to catching up with each other's lives and talking about the old times we had together.

About an hour after my first drink, my friends started to call me, asking me what I was doing that night. I told them that I was hanging out with Love, and they couldn't believe it. They had to ask to make sure it was the same one who went to school with us all of those years ago. I told them that, yes, it was. Then my friends, being the typical guys they are, asked if she and I were going to be having sex with each other.

Now me being the person I am, I just came out and asked her if she planned to have sex with me. This question didn't bother her at all. She responded with a no, so I figured my friends should come over then.

My friends said they would be over in fifteen minutes, and sure enough, they were. Once my friends walked into my room, even they couldn't believe that I had a drink in my hand. They all had to smell it and taste it just to make sure that it was real. This was about the time that she finally believed me that I had never drank before in my life. All of my friends even told her the same thing.

Right then, her mood changed. She felt she had done something wrong. She felt as if she corrupted me. My friends saw it a different way. They all figured that, if they wanted me to start drinking with them, all they would have had to do was find Love, and that would have taken care of it.

Love only stayed for about another half hour after she found out the truth. She said she had to get back to her daughter so I walked her out to her car. I looked her straight into her eyes, saying it was okay and I was completely stone sober when I was completely drunk off my ass. I hugged her and helped her get into her car. I closed the door for her and watched as she pulled out of my driveway and drove down the street into the distance.

I wondered if I would even see her again after that night or if it would be a repeat of before. I figured I should have taken that as a good-bye for now because you never know what can happen in the future.

The rest of the night was spent by having my friends drive me around everywhere during my drunken state because they thought it would be funny. All I remember from that night was thinking about Love every second and eating a lot of food from everywhere we went. I say that it turned out to be a very successful night overall.

As for now in my life, Love and I spent a lot of time together after I returned home. She even mentioned to me once that she felt like I was the only person who understood her and got her personality. She even thought that, at one time, we were almost the same person. I did everything I could to show her that I loved her. I would send flowers to her house, take her to concerts, and do almost anything for her that her heart desired. Sadly, she didn't see it the same way that I did. She decided she didn't want to be in a relationship with me and she wanted to be with someone else.

I'll be honest. I took it pretty hard, and I couldn't believe it. I don't talk to her as much as I used to. She still had the guilt of me drinking after the time we spent together. I told her not to worry about it, and if she happens to be reading this, I want to let her know that I'm doing just fine and she shouldn't feel guilty. After all of that, I can't say that I am looking for a relationship or if I ever will again. I enjoy the fact of knowing that I can go out drink, fuck, and do whatever and whenever I want to. Life is good, and now let's go back to hooker stories.

THE KOREAN BLOW JOB

My job had taken me overseas at this point, but I couldn't complain. I got to see the world. The only thing that sucked was that I didn't understand any of the foreign languages they were speaking in any of the countries I went to. China would be the first of many countries I would be at. They sent us all to Hong Kong. If you don't know where it's at, it's located near the southern part of China. The worst part was that they took us to a famous American hot spot, so it was kind of ruined for us.

The workdays went by just as they did back in the States, except we had a few translators to help us figure out things and we also had some of the people from China working with us. After all, it was their homeland, and they knew what they wanted done. The only things that sucked was having to be patient all of the time after we were used to working at a fast pace. It usually made for some long days.

They did give us a couple of days off to actually enjoy ourselves and the country during our time spent there. During the day, not much happened. Everyone would go to work and run errands, just like we do here in America, but when the nighttime hit, it was as if someone turned on the party switch and everyone knew it. The city was lit up with bright neon lights and loud music everywhere, and the smell of good food and booze flowed through the air. I could get used to this. Too bad I was only here for a couple of weeks.

The day before, our boss told me and the other guys I worked with that we would be given the next day off. Instantly, we were making plans for what we wanted to do with our day off. We even asked some of the translators what was something we should do or things we should see during our time in Hong Kong. They recommended that we get out and see the city and enjoy the beach and the nice weather during the day. After all, it was summertime. Then they told us that, if we really wanted to have some fun, we had to go visit Texas Street at night.

Instantly in my head, I thought, "Why the hell would I go to a place called Texas Street when I'm from America? I want to see Chinese stuff."

We told them thanks for the recommendations, and we headed on our way back to our hotel room after work. We got to our room and decided we would go see the beach in Hong Kong because it was supposed to be famous around the world. We also figured we would go see the aquarium that was there as well. Then everyone concluded that we would go visit this Texas Street that the translators told us about. We all set our alarms and got ready for what the next day ahead would bring us.

The alarm went off at eight o'clock, and we all got ready to see what Hong Kong was all about. We met down in the lobby of the hotel and had the front desk give us directions to the train station. The only thing bad about deciding to take a train to the beach was that everything was in Chinese so it took us forever to figure out what train to get on and what station to get off at. Finding the train to there was a whole other adventure within itself. We had to walk through what looked like an underground strip mall as all the vendors were trying to get us to buy whatever junk they were selling. It was almost like those people in big cities that put out a blanket and throw random junk on it, only to charge high prices for things they found in the trash.

After fighting past all of the vendors and successfully mapping out our journey on the subway system, we were finally on our way to the beach. The cool thing about the Chinese subway system, at least the one we were on, was that, in between stops on the subway walls, they would play a movie projected, just like you were at the theaters. It is sometimes crazy to think of all the other technologies that other countries have that we don't.

Once we all got to our stop, we broke off into groups. I would be spending the rest of the day with Psycho, one of the most interesting people I ever met, and he really did not have a care in the world. Psycho is a bigger guy, about six-foot-four, with a shaved head and usually a look of craziness on his face. Rome isn't as crazy, and Psycho still has his moments. Rome is an Italian guy who stands about six foot tall with short black hair and a seventies guy mustache. Hanging out with the two of them made the day a little more interesting.

We made our way to the main street and started following the smell of the beach water as the wind pushed it in our direction. It was the hurricane season in China, which made the waves any surfer's dream. After we finally reached the beach, taking in the sights from the city as we walked through it, Psycho and I decided to check out the aquarium while Rome headed right to the beach, only to stop and grab a couple of beers on the way.

This was probably the most interesting aquarium I had ever been to in my whole life. The whole thing was built underground. I swear with it being that close to the beach that you would think it would be a safety hazard. This aquarium also had the biggest electric eels I had ever seen in my life, but the best part was the walk-through shark tunnel. Now if the glass on the shark tunnel ever broke, I'm sure someone would be having a bad day.

It was a good way to waste the day now that Psycho and I had come back up the surface. We just had to figure out where both we and Rome were.

Now let me tell you a little about this beach. It's over three miles long, and the whole thing is set up with umbrellas of different colors signifying a different section of the beach. Finding Rome was not going to be the easiest task in the world, but we had no choice, and we started looking. You think that trying to find an American in a foreign country would be easy; however, I've had better luck trying to pet a grizzly bear. The other part that wasn't helping us was that absolutely no one spoke English, so once again, we were getting nowhere fast.

Psycho and I must have walked the beach for what seemed like forever until we finally came across a weird sight. One after one, we watch some of the Chinese lay down next to Rome as they took photos of themselves next to him. This would have been okay if Rome weren't passed out in the sand. It turned out that Rome had drank the beers he got and decided he would take a nap in the sun. I didn't see why they just didn't ask to take a picture with him, but everyone has his or her own reasons.

Psycho and I approached the passed-out Rome and asked him how the beach was and if he took any good pictures lately. He said no to the pictures with a confused look on his face, and he never stepped foot into the water. Psycho and I saw it differently with the big waves that were coming in. How could you not want to jump into the water? We were so sure enough that we ran down the beach into the water, and sure enough, the first wave that hit me threw me right back onto the sand. Talk about a good time. Throughout the water, they had lifeguards set up, saying you could go past a certain point for your own safety.

After several hours of trying to dodge waves, one guy actually bumped into me and turned around to keep apologizing to me. So to make it up to him, I told Psycho to give him a shoulder massage because I thought it would be funny. The guy took it a little differently and thought Psycho was playing some game, so the next big wave that came around, the guy jumped on my back and told me to save him. The wave hit my face and drowned me. First, he apologized to me, and then he tried to kill me. What a weird guy. I thought I had all I could take from the beach one day as we made our way back to see how Rome was doing.

Sure enough, Rome was lying out all day, trying to get his tan on. We all decided that it was time to leave the beach and to start doing some barhopping. The beach was lined with hotels all down the board, and we must have hit every single bar in every hotel along the way. Then after a while, it seemed like the night fell over the city, and sure enough, all of the bright neon lights came on, and the party was starting.

We decided that the night would be started off by trying some of the famous Korean BBQ that everyone was always talking about. The only thing was that we had to figure out what place had it due to all the signs being in Chinese. Luckily, we ran into another American that we'll call English, mainly because she was living in China as English teacher, which was perfect for us because she knew Chinese as well. English was about five-foot-five with long dark blonde hair and soft-spoken and beautiful green eyes. I don't think that her plans for the night consisted of hanging out with us, but she tagged along anyway.

English helped us find the restaurant that we were looking for, and she even joined us for dinner. The only thing sad about dinner was that the smoothies we were ordering to drink soon became more important than the food we were eating. We soon discovered that, with help from English, we had been drinking Soju the whole time without us even knowing it. Soju is a famous Korean alcohol that smells and tastes like straight grain alcohol; however, we couldn't taste it in the smoothies. I'll admit that, by the time dinner was over, I was feeling the effects big time.

We paid the bill, left the restaurant, and asked English what else there was to do for fun in the area. She recommended we check out of the local karaoke bars. I'm not really big on singing, but I figured that, if it were a bar, they would most likely have beer there and possibly more Soju. We all agreed that a karaoke bar would be the next stop on our list, but Psycho first recommended that we stop for more Soju along the way. How could I say no to that one? Our quest for Soju didn't take too long as we found out that right next to the restaurant was a liquor store carrying Soju.

Psycho ran inside, and we made our way to the karaoke bar. Once we got there, we realized it was set up a little differently. Unlike the bars here that have karaoke where it's usually one giant open area and it's most of the times held in an actual bar, this place was nothing like that. Here, you went into a room with just the group you were with. You paid to rent the room, and you paid for your drinks at the door. Once everything was paid for, we were shown to our karaoke room, where Psycho, Rome, English, and I got drunk and sang classic rock tunes until our hour was over.

Once our time at the karaoke bar was over, we made our way to the street and said our good-byes to English because she had to work the next day. We had to work, too, but we still planned to party for as long as we could. The next and last stop on our list would be the famous Texas Street that we were recommended to go to.

The three of us flagged down a cab and piled in, as we knew this would be an interesting ride.

With all of us being under the influence during this time, our cabdriver started to hate us more and more every mile he drove. Rome was hanging out the window, yelling at people for directions, trying to confuse everyone in the cars next to us. And Psycho was asking the cabdriver if he could blow a load on his face. I really don't know how the cabdriver didn't kick us out into the middle of the road that night.

The cab ride seemed as if it took forever, but that could have been due to a number of reasons. We had finally reached Texas Street to read signs that were written in English and see everyone we worked with. If I didn't know that we were in a foreign country, it would have looked like one giant block party to me. All of the bright neon lights on the signs were lighting up the street, the loud music was pouring out from the open doors to the bars, and the girls were hanging out on the front steps, asking you to come in for a drink. It was like a little piece of heaven. I could see why we were told to come here now.

Psycho, Rome, and I started walking down the street, hopping from bar to bar and trying to find one that we liked. This was the first time I had found out what a "buy me drink" girl was. If you thought the girls in America hanging out at the bars were bad, trust me. You haven't seen much yet. The "buy me drink" girls are exactly just as they sound. They work for the bar, and all they do is have you buy them drinks just so they can talk to you. They don't want much anything more to do with you than that, but you just have to keep looking.

So after we were having a tough time trying to find a bar that was decently good, we decided that we should split, and each person would take a different part of the street, trying to find just a normal bar. I walked down to the furthest part of the street and ran into Cali, another coworker of mine. Cali is about five-foot-seven with jet-black hair and a perfect tan year-round. He is also from Southern California as well. He was yelling at me, telling me with a drunk slur that he found the best bar on the whole damn street. So I figured I'd try it out.

He led me down to what must have been the last bar on the whole street. Go figure. To find the best one, you would have to walk past all of the other ones just to get to it. As soon as we walked in, I thought the whole place would be packed and the drinks would be flowing. I couldn't have been more wrong. This place was deader than disco. The only thing that impressed me when I first walked in was the horde of women that surrounded me.

They led me right to a table, sat me down, and got me a drink. This was when the fun began.

A Korean woman came back with my beer in her hand. She stood about five-foot-six with long black hair down to her ass, pale skin, a short cut top, and a pair of Daisy Dukes. Krisy, as I like to call her, as in Korean Daisy, sat right down on my lap and started a normal conversation with me in plain English. I couldn't believe it. Out of the whole time I was there, I finally found a woman who could speak English clear. She asked me the basics, starting with where I was from, what I did for a living, and if I were married, the simple things like that.

As my eyes drifted away for a second, I looked over at Cali, and I saw him having the time of his life as the girl on his lap was flirting with him and biting his neck. It looked like he was in high school all over again.

Krisy started asking me if I had found a girl that I liked while I was in China. I told her that I was still keeping my options open. I watched as she got the biggest smile on her face, took my beer away from me, and started making out with me. This was going on for a while, and I was losing track of time, but I personally didn't care at this point. All I knew, I was busy, and it was going to get better from there. Krisy then reached down, unzipped my pants, and started giving me a hand job. I'm not going to lie. I had thought I was going to sleep with someone while I was in China. I just didn't think that I would be getting a hand job in the middle of the bar. Luckily, the bar was empty so it wasn't like I had to worry about someone being a creep and staring at me.

Then of course, the twist came. Just as it seemed things were looking good, she stopped and told me that, if I wanted the rest, we had to go upstairs. Sure, I would love to go upstairs and finish the rest of this. Then Krisy told me that it was going to cost me a hundred Korean dollars. I can't remember what the exchange rate was, but I know it was good back then. So it's not like I was spending a lot. The only part that sucked now was that I didn't have the money in my wallet, so I had to go to the closest ATM and get out more money.

So I told Krisy I would be right back, and I had her give me directions to the closest ATM. I walked outside, and then I heard Cali telling me to wait for him. Cali came out of the bar and met me on the street. He then told me that his girl offered to go upstairs with her, but it was going to cost him. Now he told me that he was strapped for cash, but this was something he really wanted to do. I swear, some people. It was bad enough I paid for my own prostitutes, but now other people were asking me to pay for theirs. I started thinking why he would be asking me then, and after all, I would only be getting anything out of one of them. So why should I pay for it?

Cali told me that people checked his bank accounts and he could make any big withdrawals so people wouldn't become suspicious. I figured, if it would get him to shut up, then I would lend him the cash. So we headed on our way down the street to the ATM.

Once we got the money taken out, we rushed back to the bar as fast as we could because I was ready to get on with it already. Sure enough, waiting in the door to the bar was Krisy, waiting for me to get back. I handed Cali his money and told him to go and find his girl as I approached Krisy. Krisy asked me if I got the money and if I were ready for a good time. I told her yes as I handed her the cash. Then she grabbed me by the hand and led me upstairs.

Once I got upstairs, I couldn't believe what I was seeing. The bar and the room upstairs looked a lot nicer than the bar downstairs, almost as if they had remodeled the upstairs but could care less about the business downstairs.

As I stood there in confusion, Krisy asked me what I would like to drink, and I ordered another beer. It wasn't like I was going to be drinking much of it anyway. I was already drunk, and I would be too distracted to grab my beer in the first place. She then headed over to the bar as I saw Cali and his girl come upstairs. He asked me the same question, why the upstairs to the building looked amazing compared to the shit hole that was downstairs. I wished I would have had an answer, but I was still confused myself. Krisy then came back over with my beer as she handed it to me and told me to follow her.

Krisy then led me down a hallway with rooms on both sides. She led me right to a room that was very well lit, couches that wrapped around the room, and a giant screen TV. She told me to go and sit in the far corner of the room as she turned down the lights and took off her shirt. She then grabbed what looked like a remote and told me that I would have to pick something to help shut out the sound. I thought to myself, "This is awesome. Not only am I getting laid, but I got myself a screamer."

That was what I thought until the truth came out about the music part. It turned out she had led me into my own private karaoke room. I couldn't believe it. I just got done at a fucking karaoke bar. Why the hell would I want to sing anymore, especially while I was supposed to be having sex?

I figured that there must have been some motive to the madness as I went through and picked out every single classic rock song I wanted to listen to once again. As soon as I punched in the first song on the remote, it started playing, and she told to just keep picking songs. It wasn't until I must have picked out about ten songs that we started actually getting to it. Once again, we started making out. She started biting my neck, and then she took off my shirt. Things were finally looking good for a perfect end to the night.

Krisy then unzipped my pants. Then she reached over, grabbed a microphone, and handed it to me. Instantly in my mind, I was thinking, "You've got to be fucking kidding me."

Sure enough, she told me that I had to sing along to the music so this way the people around us thought that we were singing and not having sex. So let's recap really quick. I'm in a bar with a shitty downstairs and a nice upstairs. I just paid for a prostitute and someone else's. I'm in a foreign country, and now I'm expected to sing while having sex. I can officially say that I was taken outside of my comfort zone that night.

So I started singing into the mike as the thoughts were racing through my mind about how this was going to work. Krisy then unzipped my pants and pulled out my dick, and she started giving me a hand job and encouraged me to keep singing. Trust me. It sounds a lot easier than it sounds.

After a few minutes of her sliding her hand up and down my dick, she decided that she wanted to start sucking on my dick now. So now here I was, getting a blow job while singing classic rocks. The whole thing seemed pretty American to me, but at the same time, it all seemed very strange.

Everything was going perfectly, and it seemed like the night was going to end on a good note. That was what I thought until I heard a loud knocking come from the door, and I saw a face peeking through the window on the door.

I told Krisy that someone was at the door, and it seemed like he really wanted to get into this room. She kept assuring me that it was no one and he would go away. That would explain why the knocking got louder and the person on the other side of that door was getting more pissed by the second. Krisy continued to suck my dick, and the person at the door eventually went away. I figured I could get on with the rest of my time with Krisy. As I began to relax and go back to listening to the music and enjoying my blow job, the worst possible thing could have happened.

It turns out that the pissed-off man found the owner of the bar and demanded him to open the door to my room. The next thing I knew, the door came flying out. Krisy jumped up, pulling her mouth off my dick as she struggled to find her top. I looked at who was standing in the doorway. I couldn't believe who it was. My boss was looking at me with daggers in his eyes, yelling at me to get my clothes on and get the hell out of the room. It was kind of like getting caught masturbating by your parents. Many of the same feelings were shared in the moment. I gathered all of my clothes, put them on, and made my way down to the street below. I found something I liked doing in this country, and it got cut short. Of course that would happen to me.

Once Cali and I were on the street, our boss came storming out, asking us how stupid we could be. He couldn't believe that we had come to a foreign country and paid to sleep with someone. He then asked us what would have happened if we had caught something or if something bad would have happened, such as getting mugged or killed in an isolated area.

I then asked him how he knew we were there. It turned out that he was sitting at a bar down the street, and he watched the two of us run into the building as fast as we could. He said it made us look like we were up to something, so he felt like he had to check it out. Then I asked why he was on Texas Street if he were married. He told me to shut up and not to mention this night to anyone again. I guess I can say that my night got cut short that night.

After that, we had only spent a few more days in China, and sure enough, we kept it quite around the work area about what had happened that night. The rest of the time I was there, I never did go back to that bar. I figured, after that night and wasting my money by having my boss catch me, it wasn't worth the struggle of going back. This was only one of the first stops on the many countries we had to go to, so I figured that there would be many more.

The lessons learned from this one are:

- Don't sing while having sex because it will be too distracting.

- Make sure your boss isn't around if you are going to be doing something you shouldn't.

- Don't fall asleep at the beach if you don't want your picture taken.

- Don't pay for other people's prostitutes.

- And last, enjoy every second of something while you have the chance because you never know when it might get cut short or taken away from you.

9

THANK YOU,
PLEASE DON'T CUM AGAIN

We were all ready to leave China and move on to the next stop. After all, there is only so much a man can take of kimchi before it gets old. The last few days were spent wrapping up the last of work, getting everything together that we brought with us, and making sure that everyone was still alive. The boss and I still never did bring up the events of that night. Every time I saw him, I couldn't help but laugh because, after a while, it had its own hysterical value to it. China did bring some good times and memories, but I couldn't wait to get to the next stop.

A few days later, we were landing in our stop, and I couldn't have been happier. We had to go to Manila, which is located in the Philippines, for some more work. The Philippines were awesome with the warm weather, shining sun, palm trees, and blue water. The best part was that mostly everyone spoke English, so we didn't have the language barrier like we did in China, and the exchange rate was dirt cheap. At the time, it was one American dollar to fifty Filipino pesos. Everywhere I went, I was being treated like a millionaire even though I was nothing more than a blue-collar worker here in American. Enjoying all of this could only mean that something bad was going to happen.

Our boss gave us the same deal that he gave us in China. We would work for a couple of days and then have a day or two off to enjoy the country and take in the culture. The only thing he added into his speech this time was that he didn't want to catch any of us doing something that we shouldn't be doing. I wasn't really sure if he were saying it to me directly or if he felt guilty for the fact he got caught himself. I never did ask; nor did I really care. So we all did the exact same thing that we did before. We asked the locals where all the fun was.

All of the locals recommended a place called Mango Street. I thought to myself, "You have got to be kidding me. First, I get recommended to go to a place called Texas Street, and now I'm being told to go to a place called Mango Street. Why can't they just have normal names for their streets, like First Street or something?"

The locals told us that down on Mango Street was where all of the good bars and nightclubs were. After my last experience, I kind of had an idea of what the clubs on that street would be like. So of course, it was the one place I wanted to go to.

Everyone made a plan on how we would spend the day. Most people said they would either go sightseeing or head to the beach. Psycho and I had a different plan that, in all honesty, wasn't really the smartest idea, but I was always up for an adventure. Psycho had the idea of going out and buying some syringes and tricking everyone at work into thinking that he was a heroin-addicted rock star.

First of all, Psycho wasn't a rock star; nor was he a heroin addict. So I really wanted to see how that plan was going to work out. Another crazy thing about the Philippines is that you can walk into just about any pharmacy and get whatever you want without a prescription. This trip just seemed like it was getting worse by the second.

So after we had a plan figured out and the day was ending, I figured it was time to go to bed. After all, I couldn't wait to see how the day would unfold tomorrow. I swear it had to be one of the worst ideas I ever heard, but it just seemed too funny to pass up. The next day came, and I got out of bed in excitement, knowing I had the day off and everything that was yet to come.

I met Psycho outside, and we waved down the first cab we had seen. We had the cabdriver take us to the mall that was a few miles away. The whole cab drive cost us about twenty-five cents American, which seemed like a luxury to the driver. Once he dropped us off, we headed inside.

The mall was huge. It had about four stories with all the same name-brand stores that we had here in America. The mall made a giant circle, so getting lost almost seemed like the furthest things from my mind. After we made a half-lap to the other side of the mall, the crazy thing was that we had reached our destination. I can't say that I've been in many malls with a pharmacy in them, so it threw me off guard when I first saw it. Nothing like going to the mall and buying your shoes and then picking up some drugs along the way.

I watched Psycho dart right into the pharmacy and head straight for the counter. The pharmacy actually happened to be busy, and I couldn't believe that this many people came to the mall to get their prescriptions filled here.

As soon as Psycho approached the counter, he said he wanted twenty syringes with the smallest needle possible. I then had to ask why he got twenty syringes when it shouldn't have taken more than at least two or three to pull off what he wanted to do. Psycho had finally admitted that it wasn't going to be a joke and he really wanted to start shooting up. Now I had encouraged him that it wasn't smartest idea of all time to start doing drugs, but it wasn't smart for me to be sleeping with prostitutes either. If I had thought about that back then, I'm sure that everything would have turned out differently. Psycho then stated that, if famous rock stars did it, he should be able to do it. Well, hey. To each their own.

The pharmacy tech came back with the syringes, and then Psycho announced that it was time to go on the search for drugs, but we first had to stop for booze. Another cool thing about the Philippines is that you can buy a fifth of rum for fifty cents American. That's right. A whole fifth for only fifty cents. It's a drinker's dream come true, if you ask me. The good thing about this mall was there happened to be a liquor store on the floor right below the pharmacy. That quest didn't take us long.

After we made our round in the mall, buying up Psycho's syringes and enough rum to even put a pirate in a drunken coma, it was finally time that we left to find the drugs. Now I don't really know if drinking in public in the Philippines is even legal, but I can say that we officially did plenty of that. I thought finding drugs in a Third World country would be a lot easier than it really was.

Once we walked out of the mall, we tried asking a few of the locals where we could find any drugs to begin with, and most walked away from us and did the best they could to avoid us. Hell, I can't blame them. We probably looked like a bunch of assholes. Besides, what kind of people just ask for drugs in public other than cops?

After about an hour of failed attempts at finding any leads of where drugs might be located, I came up with a great idea. I figured that the best chance we had would be to go to the shadiest part of town and start looking there. I mean, it seemed like a good plan, and if we couldn't find any there, we probably wouldn't find it anywhere. Psycho then asked what I thought the shadiest part of town might be exactly. I had never been to the Philippines before, so I really had no clue. I was just taking a shot in that dark. I thought about it for a while and then remembered that some of the locals from work recommended Mango Street. It was the best I could think of at the time so I figured we should start there.

We hailed a cab and got inside. Then I noticed the biggest smile and laugh came from the cabdriver as we told the cabdriver our destination was Mango Street. I instantly thought to myself that we were heading in the right direction. During our short drive over to Mango Street, our cabdriver asked us if we had even been down there before. We told him that the locals recommended us. He then laughed again and told us to keep a close eye on our wallets and to make sure that we never traveled alone. The more he talked about it, the more I knew that this was the spot we needed to be. The only thing I couldn't figure out was why the locals we would meet with in these countries would keep telling us to go to the worst parts of town.

Our cab pulled up at the halfway point between the ends of the street. We paid our cabdriver and got out as we watched the cab drive off into the distance. We then started asking around, just as we did when we were at the mall. Now it was only around noon, so we still had a lot of the day to kill, and I was sure that looking for drugs wouldn't take that long at all. We were having better luck on Mango Street with our search for drugs. The only problem was that no one wanted to help us. Every shady person on the streets who looked like he or she was on drugs told us where to go, but no one wanted to take us there. All said it was too dangerous.

Now Psycho was getting pissed off because we had spent all day trying to find one thing, and we finally got close, but no one wanted to help us. Talk about a waste of time. Psycho finally decided to forget about it. He figured that, if he couldn't get drugs, he would at least get a tattoo and do something exciting while we were in the Philippines. Now that was something I could be into. The crazy thing about Mango Street is that it seems like, every time you are looking for something, it seems to be right there when you need it. Ironic, if I must say so.

Less than a block down the street, we walked right up to the tattoo parlor. The story behind what Psycho got tattooed on him kind of revolves around my tattoo. About a year before in March 2010, I got the words "prison tattoo" tattooed on my arm. This then inspired Psycho to get the words "drunk tattoo" tattooed on his leg. I'm not going to lie. It turned out looking really good when it was done. It took about six hours for both of our tattoos to get done. I got my twelfth and most current to date of my fourth pinup girls on my leg. I only speak of my tattoos because of the significance they'll play later in this story.

By the time we were done at the tattoo shop, nightfall had already come, and all of the bars were opening. The only thing bad about Mango Street that I wish someone would have told me about was all of the people that linger on the street at night. Once night comes, all of the kids and teenage girls come out, and they try to take advantage of you. By this, I mean they get one of the teenage girls to go on one side of you to get you distracted. After you are already paying attention to the girl you have your arm around and listening to her saying she wants to suck your dick, then a little kid comes up one the other side of you, reaches into your pocket, and takes whatever you got. They have this system down to a science.

So on our way to the bar, we had to fight off the arm of little kids and teenage hookers just to get anywhere on that street. The first bar we stopped at had a green sign lit up out front, and the sign read "Twins." I'm not going to lie. This sign was false advertisement. It was called

Twins because every woman in the bar was required to wear a green cocktail dress, and they all looked alike. I say it was false advertisement because none was actually twins. That can really throw off a man.

As soon as Psycho and I walked into the bar, he ran straight to the restroom as I made my way to the bar. On my way to the bar, I had a horde of ladies come up to me, asking my name and asking me for a drink while they were rubbing their hands all over me. I had gotten to the bar slowly but surely just to order my first beer for the night. Yes, by the time my tattoo was done, all of the rum I drank had worn off by this time.

I told the bartender to get me whatever the local beer was. If I would have known that this beer had a reputation for giving people the shittiest hangovers in the world, I would have never drank it. The bartender turned around, and in no time, they found their way back to me. By the time the bartender had turned around again to give me my beer, the ladies already had my clothes off, and I was completely naked in the bar.

I thought it was pretty awesome to be in a bar for less than ten minutes and already have my clothes off by a bunch of complete strangers. I'm not going to lie. You probably won't see that much in America. After I got my beer, the ladies escorted me to a table where Psycho had been sitting. They sat me down completely naked in the chair as one woman after another started coming up to me, rubbing their hands on me. Each one took a turn rubbing on me. In fact, one of the ladies asked me if I wanted to go to hell, and I wasn't quite sure how I should have responded to that question.

I had let this go on for about twenty minutes while Psycho laughed his ass off at the fact that I was already naked and I hardly even did anything. Sure enough, after a while, other people from work started coming in, amazed at what they were seeing because seeing me naked in a bar was not what they thought they would run into that night. I figured that, if other people were coming in from work, my boss was on his way, and I'd rather not have a China repeat. I pushed the girls off me and put my clothes back on, and so that fun ended quickly.

After I got all my clothes on, I asked Psycho what his plans were for the rest of the night. All he said was that he just wanted to find the drugs. I actually couldn't believe that we were back on this topic. I thought we moved on from it, but of course, I figured I would help him. So we figured that we would start asking the girls at the bar if they knew of any way they could get the drugs for us. Instantly, they all got on their phones and even got their bosses on their phones as well, trying to find some. I was thinking to myself that this was pretty cool. This country catered to everything you wanted at any time. I could have gotten real used to this.

A half hour went by, and one of the bosses of the bar came over and told us that she had a connection to a guy who was selling crack. As soon as Psycho heard this, he asked if the dealer had anything else, and they said no. This was all that the man happened to be selling. Now I wasn't quite sure what Psycho's logic was, but he said he would do meth, coke, and heroin; however, he said he would never smoke crack. I don't really see how that makes sense, but I guess everyone has some values in his life. Right then, Psycho's search for drugs ended that night.

We had spent at least two hours at Twins, and then Psycho told me he wanted to check out another bar on this street. So once again, we headed outside to face the madness of the crazies. This time, walking down the street, I might have lost my cool a little bit and yelled something to people, such as "Go die in a ditch" or "Fuck off." It would be a lot easier if that part weren't a blur, but these are the things that other people tell me about that night.

Psycho had read a sign that said "Pirates," and we wanted to check it out to see if it were anything like the one in Guam. Now I have never been to the Pirates bar in Guam, but I hear that you can pay any stripper in the place to beat up anyone that you want for a little cash. Right then, we headed down the stairs into the bar,

Now I should have thought this bar was a little shady because I had to walk down a flight of stairs to get to it and the bar was poorly lit to begin with, but I would find out soon enough. Psycho's idea of the bar was wrong. There were no strippers beating each other up, sad to say. Instead, these strippers hardly even stripped at all. All these strippers did was get onstage and show off their dance moves without taking off any clothes. To me, this seemed boring, but the bar had beer, so we decided to have a few drinks.

We took our seats at the bar, and just like the last bar, they were serving the same shitty beer. I couldn't complain though, only having to pay twenty-five cents American for it. You couldn't beat the price. Too bad that, when I got my beer this time, no girls ripped off my clothes. After the bartender handed me my beer, I turned around to watch the girls dance onstage.

Just then out of the corner of my eye, I saw Swamp on the other side of the bar, sitting with Ops. Ops got his name because everything he did had to be planned out like a special ops mission even if it were him just taking a piss. The ironic part about Ops is that he had the worst case of ADD I had ever seen. He couldn't pay attention to anything for more than a minute. Ops stands about six-foot-tall with a buzz cut, and for some strange reason, he always had his head cocked a little to the left.

I turned to Psycho and asked if he wanted to go and sit over by them, but he was too busy arguing with the bartender, saying he was a rock star and deserved free drinks. I left Psycho to his argument and made my way over to Swamp and Ops. The gang at work was still learning around this time that we shouldn't let Swamp and Ops get drunk together because something usually would get broken and they both had a fascination with sharp, shiny objects. In fact, it was pretty bad that, on Thanksgiving, we had to hide anything that could have been used as a weapon before they could get their hands on it.

I approached Swamp and Ops, and they lit up with excitement as they yelled my name loud enough for the outside to hear it. I knew they were at least buzzed by this time and having the time of their lives. I asked what they were doing here, considering the fact that both of them happened to be married. Then Ops spoke up and said they were there to execute a mission called "Take Over This Bar." I told them good luck on their plan and asked how their day was going. It turned out that they went out on Jet Skis and were chasing around and pissing off freighters for the better part of the day until Swamp decided he had to get an anniversary gift for his wife. I asked Swamp what he bought, and I knew I shouldn't have asked this question

Swamp had ordered another beer and told me that he couldn't find anything good here, so he decided to do some online shopping back at his hotel room for a minute. Swamp then told me that he found the perfect gift and was having it shipped to the house. Swamp then called his wife and told her that she had her gift on the way. Swamp then told me that he had bought her a hatchet. I asked why he bought her hatchet, and then he said it wasn't for her. It was for him, and it was the only way he could have it was if he said it was an anniversary present. I guess that's the perks of being married.

About an hour had passed by, and finally, the beer was running through me, so it was time I decided that I would take a piss. Trying to find the restroom was a challenge within itself for this bar had more hallways than a maze it seemed like. The first room I walked into, I thought it was the restroom, and it turned out that I walked into the room where all the girls get ready. My view was overtaken by half-naked girls and tits in every which direction I looked. That must be what heaven is like walking into. The weird thing was that none of the girls even cared that I was standing there. Now if that would have happened here in American, I would have gotten a lawsuit before I even made it out the door.

I eventually found my way out of this room. I couldn't really say how long I was in there for, but I'm sure it was quite some time. I asked where the restroom was, and believe it or not, I had to walk out the back door, go into the back alley, and then head up a flight of stairs just to get to it. I've seen a lot of horror movies in my time, and I'm sure this scene has been in a few of them right before a person got killed. The girls weren't lying. That really was the way to the restroom, and the best part was that I didn't get killed or raped, so that was a good thing.

I was making my way back into the bar, and I decided it was too hot to be wearing my shirt. This was the biggest mistake that I could have made. Once again referring back to my tattoos, I have two pinup girls on my shoulders and a human heart on my chest, and the most recognizable of all is the smiley face I have tattooed on my belly button. If I would have known what was going to happen later, I would have left my shirt on.

I opened the door to the bar, and the most ironic thing that could have been happened did while I was gone. Swamp, Ops, and Psycho all decided that it would have been a good idea to take off their shirts as well. Swamp and Ops did it because they wanted to show the girls what strippers in America do all while dancing onstage, and Psycho was trying to prove his point more that he was a rock star. Psycho even went to the point of asking one of the girls for makeup so he could apply it to his face, like how most eighties rock bands used to do.

One of the waitresses working at the bar approached me. She told me that my friends and I were pretty crazy. I couldn't help but think in my head that she really had no idea. She then asked me if I liked any of the girls from the bar. I'm not going to lie. The whole time I had been there, I wasn't really paying much attention to the girls, so I started looking around and told the waitress that some of the girls looked pretty good. Then she said the magic words. She told me, if I were interested in any, I could pay for their time and take them to the hotel. Right then, I started looking for the one I wanted.

I walked around the whole bar and saw women of all shapes and sizes. Some were smaller than others were, while some were bigger than others were. Then I laid my eyes on the one I wanted. She had just walked onstage, and the music started. I turned my head to see this girl who had a bob haircut with blonde highlights, a light tan skin complexion, and a tight body. I went back over to the waitress and asked her how I went about getting the girl onstage to go with me.

She said all I had to do was talk to the mama-san, the woman in charge of all the girls. She has usually been in the business for so long that most of them look ancient. She ran the books and made sure she knew where every girl was at all times. Basically, you can call her the pimp.

I thanked the waitress for helping me, and I walked over to the mama-san. I can't say I ever met anyone more excited in my life than this old woman. She knew exactly what I wanted as soon as I approached her, and I told her the girl onstage dancing right now with the short hair. Mama-san looked at me, smiled, and then told me that she was one of the bar's best girls. Now when someone says this, it kind of ruins the whole mood because it makes the girl sound like she's used up. And then I want nothing to do with her. This was not the case in this situation. Instead, I was drunk, and I knew what I wanted.

I asked the mama-san how much it was going to cost me. She told me that it cost thirty dollars American.

Now on a side note, if you ever pay anything below a hundred dollars here in the States, just be advised that you're probably getting more than what you bargained for. I can officially say that, in the States, I've never paid anything below $150, and I turned out clean. Since I was in a different country, it was the right price.

As soon as I handed the mama-san the money, she waved it in the air to one of the bouncers and called him over. The bouncer came rushing across the bar instantly at the demand of the mama-san. Once he approached us, the mama-san whispered something in his ear, and the bouncer ran again right to the stage to tell the girl to get off and get ready.

The mama-san instructed me to sit and wait at the bar and said it would only take a few minutes. I walked over to Psycho and told him I would be leaving for a while to go have sex. I'm not going to lie. I didn't really ever hide it from anyone, but no one even really cared. He said okay and went back to his argument. Yes, his rock star argument went on for quite some time that night. I walked back over to the mama-san, sat down, and waited.

About fifteen minutes went by, and the bouncer had come back over this time with the girl onstage. I asked for her name. She told me it was Cherry. I couldn't told if this were her stage name or her real name, but it seemed to fit her pretty well. The bouncer then escorted us up the stairs to the street.

Luckily since I had a bouncer with me, the kids and teenagers stayed away from me this time. The bouncer hailed a cab, and Cherry and I climbed in as the bouncer told the cabdriver where to go and handed him money. Now when I first got in the cab, I didn't think it was going to turn out the way it did. So here it goes.

The cab ride lasted about ten minutes until we reached our destination, and I asked Cherry a little bit about her life. She told me that she was twenty years old and said she grew up in a small farm town just on the outskirts of the city of Manila. She told me she moved to the city about six months ago when she started working at the bar. I figured it was just any other story.

The cab pulled up to the hotel but drove into the underground parking structure. The whole thing started giving me a weird vibe, so I started being on my guard. Once the cab was parked, a small Filipino man opened Cherry's door and helped her out as I got out on my side of the cab. He then shut the door behind her. I shut mine, and the cabdriver drove off. The man then led us to the bottom of a stairwell and told us to wait. The more

I stood there, the more I got an uneasy feeling building up in my gut, and paranoia started setting in. I finally turned to Cherry and asked her if this were a setup. She kept reassuring me that it wasn't.

The man had come back after about five minutes of waiting and told us he would show us to our room. As soon as he placed his foot on the first step, I grabbed him by his arm and asked him if I were going to get jumped when I got to the room, and he told me no. I then reassured him that, if I did get jumped, I was going to kick his ass first. I could then see the fear in his eyes as he laughed it off. I took that as a warning sign as we made our way up the stairs.

The climb had seemed like it took forever mostly because I had a decent amount of alcohol in me at the time, but we finally arrived at the door to our room. The man had opened the door, and just because of his laugh earlier, I grabbed the man and threw him in the room as soon as he opened it. I then asked him again if I were being set up. Now I could tell I had the man's attention. He was being honest. There was no setup, but the uneasy feeling still wasn't going away. I told the man to get out of the room and shut the door behind him.

The room was set up more like a luxury apartment. It looked like a place that a modern family here in America would live in, complete with wax fruit on the table. It was almost like I stepped into a teleport to go back home. The only other thing that stuck out in this room was the giant mirror that covered the whole wall next to the bed in the bedroom. At the time, I thought it was cool. Now I look back and think I was probably being watched, recorded, or something. As far as I know, I'm on the Internet somewhere, having sex with this girl, but I haven't seen anything yet, so it's highly unlikely.

The second we got into the bedroom, I ripped all of the covers off the bed and then turned around to get Cherry's clothes off her. She then climbed on top of the bed, and I then took off my clothes. I got on top of the bed, and the fun began. I was finding out why the mama-san said she was one of the bar's best girls. This girl was the most flexible thing I had ever gotten my hands on. I remember having her knees to her ears and her feet behind her head and even rolling her up into a ball. Hell, I could have married a girl like that.

Once I was done, all I could think about was how flexible Cherry was and how badly I wanted to go to sleep because she pretty much drained me of all my energy. Cherry then got off the bed and started putting on her clothes. I asked where she was going. She told me that, after I came, time was up and we had to leave. I'm not going to lie. That rule sucks.

So I followed suit and put my clothes back on. Then the uneasy feeling started coming back to me. I then turned to Cherry and asked if I were going to get jumped as soon as I walked out the door to the room or after I got to the bottom of the stairs. She told me no, so I went to reassure her.

And she cut me off and said, "Yeah, I know. You'll kick their asses."

I thought, "My girl, she knows me so well."

We left the room and made our way to the bottom of the staircase, and the short Filipino man was standing there, almost as if he were waiting for us. He then told us that he was going to get a cab, and we would be on our way. Then I did something I usually don't do. I'm going to warn you right now that what I did next might be considered a little unethical, but I felt I did it for the better, and some people even view me as a hero for doing so. I'll let you be the judge.

In many foreign countries, most schools, if not all, require the student to wear uniforms to school. To me, this symbolizes structure in life, and it shows responsibility.

So I turned to Cherry and asked her how she got into all of this. She didn't respond. I then asked if she were required to wear a uniform to school. She told me yes. I then asked why she didn't go to college. She told me that she couldn't afford it. I then asked her how she got into the bar business. The thing she told me next blew my mind. This was where the uneasy feeling was coming from.

Cherry told me that life wasn't as easy as I thought it was and she had to make sacrifices. Apparently, a few men approached Cherry one day and told her that they could help take care of her as long as she was willing to do what they wanted her to do. Cherry felt she didn't have any choice, so she decided to go with the men, not knowing what she was getting into.

The men then put her to work, but it's not the kind of work anyone should be forced to do. I couldn't believe what I just heard, and right then, I lost it. I guess this is where some of my values come into play. I'm all for the freelance prostitutes, and I believe that, if it is someone's own decision to get into it, hey, more power to her. The second that someone forces you to do this, it becomes a different story. It's just like stripping or getting into porn because someone is making you do it. It's a good life lesson that can be adapted to everyday life. I can say that forcing someone to do like this is probably one of the easiest ways to set me off.

After Cherry got done telling me the story, she could see the anger in my eyes and asked me if she could go home in a different cab. I handed her some more and told her to have a good night. I told her it was going to be a rough day at work the next day. She walked away from me, and I never heard from her again.

Then the short Filipino man came back over to me to let me know he got me a cab. I got into the cab with only one thing on my mind. I told the cabdriver to drive as fast as he could. He laid on the pedal and got me back to the bar in five minutes. I ran down the stairs and plowed right through the door. By this time, Swamp and Spence had already left. Psycho was now over by the pool table, playing pool with some random guy he had been arguing with all night.

Just then, as I took a look around for the mama-san, the same waitress from before approached me and asked me how it went. I looked at her and demanded to speak to the mama-san. She pointed me in the mama-san's direction. I then told her to get out of my face and said I was disgusted with how the bar was run.

I marched right over to the mama-san, and I did something I never thought I would do. I grabbed her by her arm and yelled at her, telling her to get her shit straight. I demanded to know who the men were that bought Cherry to this bar. Just then, she pulled her arm back from me and told me that she had a business to run and she couldn't hand out that information. It was almost as if she knew exactly the reason why I was pissed off.

I demanded again, and she told me to get out of the bar. By this time, the bar got quiet because of the yelling that was going on. The last words I said to her were that, if she didn't have the men in the bar by midnight the next night, I would come back and take care of the damn bar myself.

Just then, I felt someone big grab me and start to carry me away. I kept thinking to myself that I was going to have to fight the bouncer once I got outside. I was carried up the stairs, let go, and pushed out the door. I turned around to see Psycho laughing his ass off, and I couldn't figure out why he was laughing.

Psycho signaled a cab and told me to get in. He then told the cabdriver to floor it and get us back to the hotel as soon as possible, all the while still laughing. On the ride back, Psycho kept continuing to laugh the whole ride while I remained pissed.

At one point, the cabdriver stopped at a red light, and Psycho asked why he stopped. The cabdriver said that, if he ran it, the fine would be twenty dollars American. So Psycho handed him a twenty-dollar bill, and the driver blew through it. Talk about a crazy ride.

The cab dropped us off right where we were staying and drove away. Psycho then told me the reason why he had been laughing the whole time. He said he had never seen anyone do something so crazy in his life. He told me how screwed I was, not at work but in the Philippines. He told me that my tattoos were very recognizable and I had my shirt off most of the night. He then explained how, in order for these bars to remain open, they had to pay fees to some agency and I should have recognized that they were all on the same street.

He explained that, by now, all of the bar knew who I was and they were probably looking out for me. Now if I would have known that, I would not have gotten myself into this much of a world of shit. I most likely would have thought about what I was doing before I did it.

The rest of our time spent in Manila, I kept a close eye over my shoulder, thinking that at any minute it could have been my last. Luckily for me, we only had one more day left there before it was time for us to leave anyway, so it wasn't too bad for me.

I do, however, have an aunt who is Filipina, and I told her the story one day. She highly advised that I not go back, for I might not be leaving alive next time. I can't believe it. At the age of twenty, I was already told not to go back to a country. I can check that off my list now.

To this day, sometimes when I meet new people, for my own safety, I ask if they know any Filipinos. I can't say for sure if there are any out there looking for me, but I do know for sure that I did piss off a group of people that day. Like I said earlier, some people view me as a hero for what I did, but then again, you can be the judge on that one.

The lessons learned on this one:

- If you going to stand up for what you believe in, make sure you have everything planned before you do it.

- Don't take your shirt off in places you don't want people remembering you.

- Also, get all the facts before you pay for something.

THAILAND: THE LAND OF FREEDOM

This is probably the longest story in this book because it takes place over a couple of days and includes multiple stories. You have most likely heard some rumors, read some stories, and even seen some movie about what Thailand is like. I can tell you from firsthand experience that everything you know about Thailand is absolutely true, and it is probably one of the greatest places on earth. I believe everyone should check it out and create his or her own Thailand adventure. As for now, sit back, get comfy, and enjoy the ride.

During our transit from the Philippines to Thailand, I couldn't stop thinking about the people I probably pissed off back there and if they were ever going to come find me. I eventually started putting it behind me and thought only of the road ahead. The stop we were making was in Pattay Beach, Thailand, a city located on the west side of the country right along the coast of the water. It's famous for its Jomtien Beach, making it a huge tourist hot spot drawing in all kinds of walks of life from all around the world. Some love this place so much that they end up staying and never leaving. Hell, I can't blame them.

We arrived in Thailand around midafternoon that day. Once again, our boss gave us the usual talk about being careful, respecting the country, and not doing anything to get ourselves killed. The only thing about this speech was that he kept it short and to the point because he knew exactly what Thailand was like, and he knew he couldn't stop anything that was going to happen.

After he gave us the speech, we had to do the usual setup and check-in work to make sure everything would be good to go for the days ahead. The time we spent setting up seemed as if it were dragging by and they only brought us to Thailand to tease us about the things we could be doing. Soon enough, the boss came by and finally cut us loose for the night. His only words of advice were for us to "come back in one piece."

I chose to hang out with Dick, Spark, and Tea. Spark is from Florida and often dressed in tall T-shirts and basketball jerseys. He had a buzz cut and bright diamond earrings along with a hard-ass attitude from time to time. Tea is from California, but he was originally born and raised in China. He didn't talk much and kept to himself for the most part. The four of us departed from work and started an adventure for that day that I wouldn't soon remember.

We hopped on the bus that took us into the city. Every time we passed one of the shops on the side of the road, the vendors would almost try to throw themselves in front of the bus, trying to get the bus to stop. We finally reached the drop-off point and the Pattay Beach hotel right behind the big bar district. I'm assuming this spot was chosen so anyone could find his way back when he was drunk. Just follow the street full of bars, and it will take you right there.

As soon as we stepped off the bus, the first order of business was to start finding beer. Luckily being dropped off into the center of everything, it wasn't too hard to find. Instead of going to a bar, we figured we would just head to the nearest gas station and grab some beer to go and do some sightseeing. This was the part where I messed up. Since the rest of the world is on the metric system, I failed to realize that the beer was measured in liters instead of ounces, and yeah, the ounces will sneak up on you.

After we left the gas station, we flagged down a tuk-tuk, a type of cab that looks almost like someone put a bed of a truck with a cap and slapped it onto the back of a scooter. As the tuk-tuk driver pulled over, another man hopped out of the passenger seat. He had dark skin, and he was wearing a baseball hat backward, making him look like your typical street con artist. He tried to swindle us a deal so he could drive us around all day this way, saying we wouldn't get a better offer from anyone else in the city. We each offered to pay him two dollars to drive us around all day. With the conversion rate, the man was making over three hundred in Thai money. Talk about a good payday.

All four of us hopped into the back of the tuk-tuk, along with the man who got out of the passenger seat. And we started driving off into the countryside. During our drive, while trying to figure out what we should see first, the man kept recommending where we should go to.

They do this because, every time they go to one of these places, if the tourist spends money there, then the tuk-tuk drive gets a kickback, making more money off you. Talk about a good scam system.

The only thing that was on my mind was trying to get more beer because my liter was disappearing quicker than I could comprehend what I was drinking. The cool thing about this tuk-tuk ride was that, if we ever needed to make a beer stop, all we had to do was smack the side of the tuk-tuk, and we would instantly pull over for more beer.

We must have made three different stops for beer before we decided what our first stop would actually be. We decided that we would start at the zoo because the zoos in Thailand let you pet just about any animal you want there. Talk about getting in touch with nature. On the way to the zoo, I started to feel the beer hit me, for I had just taken down three liters and the night was just beginning. I probably should have slowed down, but I didn't think the night would have been as good as it was if I stopped drinking so early.

We made it to the zoo to find out that the zoo was already closed, and that pretty much ruined all of the plans we had with that. So we concluded that, if we were going to be doing all of the drinking that we planned on doing that night, we should stop and get some food in our system. We told the tuk-tuk to get us somewhere the locals eat, and sure enough, he did.

The restaurant first scared the shit out of me when we got there because it looked like one of the places that might be locked up aboard. It was either all of the alcohol hitting me or paranoia. I seriously thought that we were going to get kidnapped and strapped with drugs and be told to fly them back into America. It was a good thing that this never happened to us. Getting inside of the restaurant was a walk within its own because we had to walk down a long hallway to get to it.

Halfway down the hallway, a set of wheelchairs was up against the wall. I told Spark to get in one of the wheelchairs because I felt this walk was going to take forever and he should save his energy. I told him to get in the wheelchair mostly because I thought it would be funny, and it was.

Once inside of the restaurant, it opened up into a nice patio that was sitting right on the waterfront with a view we only see in magazines. This restaurant was unique because they caught all of their seafood fresh that morning and would put it into these giant fish tanks that we had to walk past in order to get to our table. Anything we wanted out of the fish tanks, all we had to do was take a net and scoop it out. The cooks would then take it into the back, kill it, and serve it to us. We don't get much service like that here in America.

During our walk to our table, I remember there being a set of stairs that we had to climb, and Spark got out of the wheelchair and carried it up the stair behind him, only to get back into it at the top of the steps. The look on the waiter's face was priceless as Spark and me both sat there and said it was a miracle that he could walk. Then Spark jumped out of the wheelchair, felt his legs, said he could walk, and then sat right back down in the wheelchair. And he said he needed to be wheeled to the table. I don't blame him. It was probably the best seat in the house.

Finally sitting down at our table, they asked us what we wanted to drink. Spark, not thinking, forgot that all the beer was measured in liters and ordered everyone a beer. And sure enough, they brought out four liters of beer and four glasses. They'll get you with this as well because the waiter or waitress will stand by your table the whole time, and every time your glass gets low and you're not looking, they fill your glass back up. Tea wasn't drinking with us this day, and I didn't blame him because someone had to get us back. This can both be really good or really bad.

At some point during this meal, the alcohol started to hit all of us. What I do remember from this meal, I ate fried rice out of a pineapple and hit on some Australian women. I'm not going to lie. Australia has the hottest women in the world, hands down. At some point, I did hit on the manager of the restaurant as well, who told me to stop because she was a tranny. It wasn't my proudest moment, but hey, who am I to judge?

After the restaurant, we decided to head back to the bar district where the bus dropped us off at. On the way back, our tuk-tuk driver decided he was a going to make a detour with us and stop by the souvenir shop. This happened to be one of the places I spoke about earlier, where, if we bought anything, the driver would have gotten a kickback. The good thing about this store was they had more beer, which was starting to become a bad sign for me because everything was starting to become a daze to me.

While we were stopped at the souvenir shop, I did look at engagement rings because, at the time, I thought I was going to get married to AT. Looking back at it now, I'm glad that Spark was able to talk me out of it. In truth,

Spark was going through a rough path with his wife, and in the end, they split up. From what I've heard, he's a lot happier now and living a better life anyway.

After the quick stop at the souvenir shop, we all decided that we were going to do something that we had only heard about, the pussy show. The pussy show consists of different women going onstage and doing different things with their vaginas. It's amazing the things these women can do.

On our drive over to the pussy show, I spent most of the drive hanging out of the back of the tuk-tuk, yelling at random cars driving by, having the time of my life. It was probably not the smartest idea, but it was a good time.

Our tuk-tuk finally arrived at the pussy show, and we were escorted into a poorly lit building. Now the thing that threw me off was the fact that so many Thai people actually showed up to watch this themselves. You would think that it would mainly be a tourist attraction and we would be the only people there, but hey, I've been wrong before.

Security made us go through a pat-down before we could go inside and take our seats, and they made us put anything that could stall the show into a locker. Once past the checkpoint, they handed us our one free beer and showed us to our seats, and the show began.

During the show, they kept taking volunteers from the audience, and of course us being the most drunk and the only people who didn't know what we were in for, we volunteered for everything and anything we could. The first thing they did was ask for four of us to go onstage and hold balloons. Sure enough, all four of us went onstage. Each one of us held a separate balloon, and one woman lay on the floor in front of us and aimed her vagina up in the aim, right in my direction. Within a few seconds, the balloon I was holding was popped. The lady shot a dart out of her vagina and popped all four balloons. Now if I hadn't seen it for myself, I wouldn't have believed it.

I kept trying to stay onstage and volunteer for anything I could, but security eventually forced me into my seat. Once security walked away, I made my way back to the stage. The women on stage had no choice after a while and finally gave in to let me volunteer again. For the next stunt, they handed me a basket and told me to go and stand out into the crowed. The lady laid on the stage again, took a banana, unpeeled it, and shoved it right up her vagina. Once she was ready, she aimed her vagina and fired away. The banana missed my basket and fell on the floor. I picked it up anyway and ate it. Hey, you know what they say. When you are in Thailand, go crazy. Actually, no one says that.

Now this is the last thing I remember from the night before blacking out and fading in and out for the rest of the night. Two women were onstage, and they both separated their legs. And one pulled razor blades out of her vagina, and the other pulled needles out of hers. No, what I did wasn't the smartest idea because I walked up to the stage, grabbed the needles, and stabbed myself right in the arm. I heard a huge grasp go over the crowd, and then I blacked out. Don't worry. I blacked out from the alcohol, not the needle.

The rest of that night, I spent it in a drunken haze of coming to and blacking out again in spurts, so these are the stories I've compiled from everyone else that night. Everyone said that, after I stabbed myself, I ran to the bathroom and started puking. This caused us to get kicked out, and then I threw up all over our tuk-tuk driver once we got outside. I felt bad for the guy after I heard that. We all piled back into the tuk-tuk, and we were driven back to the bar district where the bus dropped us off at. The sky was dark, and the street was lit up and looked like the Vegas Strip does at night.

Because we had so many bars to choose from, it was hard to make a decision to start at. So instead of wasting time, I took off running down the street, slapping every single girl on the ass that I could. Eventually, everyone caught up to me and dragged me into a bar to get me off the street. We ended up in a go-go bar, which is kind of like a strip club, except the girls don't take their clothes off. Once in the bar, I tried to order more beer to drink, and everyone kept telling the waitress to cut me off and give me nothing but water, so that was what was brought to me. Sadly, anything at this point was coming right back up.

After taking down several glasses of water and throwing them back up, I passed out at the table I was sitting at. Along came one of the go-go girls and lifted my head up so she could clean off the puke around my mouth. I wasn't quite sure who this girl was right away or what she wanted with me, so I swatted at her and told her to get away from me. After I watched her walk away, I put my head back down and passed out for quite some time.

At some point when I was passed out, I missed one of the funniest things in the world, and it still upsets me to this day that I missed this. Tea had never been with a women, and as far I as I knew, he actually never masturbated himself, so he suffered from premature ejaculation. One of the girls at the bar decided that she wanted to get his attention and start dancing with him. She started grinding up against his dick, and sure enough, he came in his pants within a matter of minutes. The part that was better than this was the fact the girl stopped suddenly from grinding on him, turned around, and grabbed his dick just to make sure. Then she called him out in the middle of the bar to let everyone know that he came in his pants. That was the part that I'm upset I missed this whole thing, but everyone told me that it was the funniest thing he had ever seen.

Everyone spent a few hours at this bar, and before too long, it was getting time to head back to where we were staying. Now I can't confirm who did this to me due to my drunken stupor, the weird part was that Dick was always the person to find me in the places I ended up. He woke me up and told me that it was time to go. By this time, I couldn't walk by myself, so I needed help getting out of the bar. Now everyone who was carrying me out of the bar took me to the street and realized that no one was following them. And they decided that they wanted to drop me and leave me for dead on a busy street in Thailand. Yeah, talk about having the time of your life, and this isn't the first or last time someone has dropped me off in a random place while I was too drunk. In fact, it started to become fad with everyone I worked with.

I'm going to sidetrack here and tell you this story really quick. One time earlier than this during our time of travel, we were in Malaysia when I got left for dead. In fact, it was the first time it ever happened. I had too much to drink that night due to the fact I didn't know my limit because I just started drinking no longer than a month before this happened. I fell asleep on the beach, and then I got woken up a few hours later by Swamp, telling me that everyone headed back to the bar. After a few seconds of talking to Swamp to figure out what was going on, I rolled over into the sand and instantly started throwing up.

Not long after the puke started coming, Dick came running down to the beach to check and see if I were okay. Once he saw me puking, he decided it was a good idea to feed me chips to help settle my stomach, but it wasn't working, so he stopped. Once I stopped throwing up, he told Swamp to take me down to the water so I could get the puke off my face.

Sure enough, Swamp, being the tank he is, picked me up and carried me into the ocean. The only problem was that he left me in the ocean and walked back into the bar. Now here I was floating facedown in the water, choking to death, unable to do anything about it because of my drunken state.

I can't say for sure how long I was in the water, but Dick eventually came running down and pulled me back onto the beach. Apparently, what happened was that, as soon as Swamp walked back into the bar, everyone asked me where I was. Swamp told everyone I was fine and pointed out that I was facedown in the water, as if it were a normal thing. This was when Dick realized that I was most likely dying and came down to help me out of the water. Now I was really glad I didn't need mouth-to-mouth because then I probably would have killed myself.

Once everyone from the bar checked me out, all carried me back into the bar and set me down in a chair. I fell asleep instantly, and I was out for another few hours. I got woken up by Dick, telling me it was time to go, and I once again stated throwing up as soon as I came to. The best part was that someone started taking pictures of me while I was throwing up, and security was getting pissed so they kicked us out as if we weren't leaving anyway.

Once outside the front doors of the bar, we got into a cab that took us back to the mall where the bus was to pick us up and take us back to where we were staying. Once we reached the mall, everyone had different plans for me. They walked me over to the steps of the mall and left me there outside the mall while everyone else ran into the mall. So not only did I get left for dead, facedown in the water earlier that night, I got left for dead a second time that night on the steps to some random mall in Malaysia. Why I'm not dead and somehow survived that night, I'll never have any idea of how that miracle happened.

Not long after being dropped on the steps to the mall, security came over and woke me up to tell me that I couldn't sleep on the steps. If only they knew that I wasn't intentionally doing it, do you think they would have left me alone? Probably not. All right back to Thailand.

So there I was, facedown in the middle of the street, outside of some random bar yet again. Sure enough, Dick came running out of the bar not long after to find out where I was and to see what kind of condition I was in. At this point, I came back to and wasn't blacked out for a few minutes. Dick, Spark, and Tea were all standing around me, trying to figure out why I was laying down in the street. I had no idea why I was there, and I was not sure if I did know why I would have had a great explanation for why I was there.

The last thing I remember was Dick yelling at me, telling me that, if I were going to be acting like that, he didn't want to party with me ever again. The last thought on my mind was debating if that were a good or bad thing, and then I went back to being blacked out. I started throwing up again, and everyone waited until I was good to go. Once all of the puke came out of me, they picked me up and put me back into the same tuk-tuk that was driving us around all day. Now if I were the driver of that tuk-tuk and one of my passengers threw up on me, I would have left his ass where he was and never driven him around again, but I guess the guy couldn't pass up the money.

Now this was when the tuk-tuk driver fucked us, and it was probably his revenge for me throwing up on him, or maybe he was just confused. Now at the time, we didn't know how close the bar was to the bus stop that we originally arrived at. If we had known that, we would have just walked to the bus stop and called it a day. Instead, the tuk-tuk driver drove us to the next city over and drove us to some random hotel that we knew nothing about. This fucked us because it made us late for the last bus, and we almost didn't make it back in time.

Outside the gates to the wrong hotel, I came back to listening to everyone yell at the tuk-tuk driver, saying it was the wrong hotel. Due to my current state, I could have cared less where I was just as long as I wasn't being left for dead again. I figured everything was fine. Shortly after all of the yelling, I blacked out yet again. At this point, everyone was freaking out more because all had no idea where we were or how long it would take us to get back to the other hotel and if we would be able to make the last bus before it departed.

So the tuk-tuk driver turned around and drove back through the dark countryside, heading back to the right hotel. Now if I weren't blacked out, I probably would have thought that this driver was taking us for a ride and was most likely going to kill us, but the good thing was that it never happened. Finally, we got back to the right hotel, and everyone pulled me out of the tuk-tuk. We sent the nightmare of a driver on his way, and we never saw him again.

We ran inside to where the bus coordinator was to ask if we missed the last bus, and sure enough, we did. He tried to help us out by getting us back somehow, and he insisted that we just chill and hang out for a minute. I then came back out to and threatened to kick his ass if he were lying to me, and I started punching the wall and the ground, telling him that, if he were wrong, I was going to replace the walls with his face. I then again blacked out.

He recommended that we get something to eat and pointed at a pizza restaurant, telling us to get some food. We all walked over to the restaurant, ordered a large pizza, and took it back to the bus stop with us. Again, everyone failed to realize that, after I've been drinking, the worst thing I could do is consume anything of any sort because I was going to throw it right back up. Sure enough, everyone kept trying to force food down my throat. After I ate the slice of pizza they made me eat, I started throwing up all over the bus parking lot. Talk about good times.

I swear I threw up enough times to make a bulimic person reconsider what he or she is doing. The bus finally came back, and we all climbed on. I took a seat at the back of the bus and lay down, and not too long after, the puke started flowing. I was told the next day that my puke managed to travel all the way from the back of the bus to the front door of the bus. That has to be a record of some sort. Luckily, this was the last time I threw up that night, and we started our departure back.

We reached the drop-off point, and Tea worked me up. And at this point, I came to and was good for the rest of the time. Like I said, what happened during the few hours I was blacked out, I wasn't quite sure, but that was all the information I gathered from what everyone else told me. What Tea told me was not what I wanted to hear after he woke me up.

The first words out of Tea's mouth were, "I can't find Dick."

I told him that Dick was most likely passed out somewhere and told him to look again. Tea came back a few minutes later and told me that he couldn't find Dick. I thought to myself that he had to be joking. So I got up out of my seat and checked myself, and I couldn't believe it, but he was right. We lost Dick, and the sad part was that he wasn't even the one who was that drunk. I kept thinking to myself, "How could we lose a person who was with us the whole time?" I knew they were going to ask questions the next day at work, and all I could think about was the shit storm that was going to rain down on us from the boss.

We told the first supervisor that we found that we lost Dick. Luckily for us, someone found Dick and already contacted everyone, telling all that Dick fell asleep and missed the trip back, but he was in safe hands. It was good to know he wasn't dead, but at the same time, how does a person who wasn't that drunk mess up that badly? They told me that I was going to follow him, but someone grabbed me and led me into the right direction so I would make it back to where I was supposed to be.

I fell asleep that night, not remembering most of the night but knowing I had a good time. And the best part was that was only the first night, and we were there for three more days. I knew it was only to get better from there on out. So yeah, don't worry. That was only day one. The hookers are yet to come.

I woke up the next day, and the best part was that I had no hangover. I guess it was because everything came out of me and there was nothing left to make me feel like shit the next day. I couldn't wait to get out and explore the city some more and try to pick up the pieces that I didn't remember from the night before. I looked for the first group of people who were heading out, and sure enough, I would find myself attached to a group with Old and Ops. At least I knew that neither of these two would leave me for dead.

We got ready and hopped on the first bus that was heading back into town to start our adventure for the day. Once we got dropped off at the same hotel that the bus dropped us off and picked us up the day before, our first order of business was to find a cab. Today, we figured that we would avoid all tuk-tuk and shady cabdrivers due to my experience from the night before.

Now, all of these cabdrivers like to do what I call hawking. They all sit and wait by either the pickup of the bus drop-off point. If they are at the bus pickup point, they will try to get you to agree to riding with them, and then they will follow the bus into town. If you choose to hop on a bus, at the drop-off point, you get swarmed with twenty different people trying to make you an offer. It's almost like a group of hawks flying over there next, preying and just waiting to strike.

Ops decided he would use his awesome negotiating skills and get a good deal. The cabdriver he found wasn't all that shady. In fact, the guy looked more like a hippie then anything. He had long black hair and jeans with holes in them, and he even dressed to impress with his sandals. He said he would drive us around all day for two dollars from each of us, and I recorded him on video agreeing to it in case he decided to screw us over later in the night, which did happen at one point during this time we spent traveling. Ops really scored with this cab because it was an actual car this time and had air-conditioning in it. This happened to be a newfound luxury in Thailand.

The three of us got into the cab and told the driver to just start driving with no real point of destination right away. The only thing on my mind today was to sleep with at least one prostitute while I was in Thailand. How could I pass up this opportunity? I mean, come on. I was in Thailand, the sex capital of the world. I had to experience it. Ops and Old always had this thing for going to the beach every time we went somewhere, so it was most likely that you could find them there, and that would happen to turn into the first stop on our list for today.

Now the beach probably wasn't the smartest idea of going to on this particular day due to the fact that a big storm was coming in that night and it caused the waves to grow to a size that could most likely swallow a building whole. This didn't bother Ops or Old once bit. Once the cabdriver pulled up to the beach, the two of them hopped out of the cab and ran immediately right into the water. I stayed behind to talk and get a few pictures of the beach, and then the cabdriver offered to take pictures of me. I took him up of the offer, and this wouldn't be the only time that day that he would take pictures of me. Luckily, they were on my camera; otherwise, I would have thought the guy was stalking me.

The cabdriver snapped a few pictures of me and handed me back my camera after I started to talk places with him. Most of the cabdrivers in Thailand keep flyers and other forms of advertisement in their car of places of interest. I told the cabdriver the one thing that was on my mind, where I could find a good hooker. He opened the front passenger door to his car, reached into his glove compartment, pulled out all the info he had on places, and told me to take my pick of where I would like to go.

Having so many options and the flyers grabbing my attention so much, it was hard to choose. They all looked so good, showing pictures of the girls they had working there and the size of the room they offered. I swear it could make anyone interested in stopping by to check it out. I asked him which one most people recommended, and he pointed out a flyer to a place called Angel. Angel was located right in the heart of Jomtien Beach, and it was rated the number-one brothel in Pattay Beach. I figured it was good enough for me and told him to take me there at some point today.

Not long after our conversation, Ops and Old came running out of the water and back to the cab, both determining that waves were too much to handle at the current time. So we were on to the next stop that day. The feeling of hunger was overtaking everyone, especially me since I hadn't had anything in my stomach since yesterday and it all came right back out of me.

We told the cabdriver to take us to a place that he recommended. I should have known better than to say that because the drive felt like forever and he took us to the same damn restaurant I was at the day before. I should have known it was a kickback place.

Once we got to the restaurant (and I'm not going to lie), it kind of pissed me off a little bit knowing that all of the cabdrivers bring all of the tourists here just to make some extra cash out of everyone. Not long after I got in the restaurant, the manager, AKA the tranny, approached me and asked me how I was still alive. She told me that I was so drunk the day before that I had no idea what I was doing, and then she tried to serve me more beer. I felt I would take it a little smarter today and not get so drunk right away because I wanted to remember at least some of my time spent in Thailand.

We sat down at our table, and I explained exactly what was going on to Ops and Old with this restaurant and said we had to be careful where the cabdriver took us because he was getting more money out of us than what we originally offered. I didn't feel like leaving because we were already here, and I was afraid of how long the drive might be to get to another restaurant, so we decided to stay. I ordered the same thing I got the day before, fried rice served in a pineapple. I'm not going to lie. The whole time I spent over in Southeast Asia, the only thing I trusted eating was rice.

During the meal, I told Ops and Old my plans for after we left, and I told them that I already confirmed them with the cabdriver. Neither one of them really cared.

In fact, they laughed at the idea and asked if I were going to do it in every country we visited. Honestly yes, that was my plan even though it didn't work out that way because they aren't all as welcoming about the idea like Thailand and the Philippines. They made their plans of agreeing to find a bar close by after I got dropped off, and the thought didn't bother me. It's not like I was going to be spending all day there anyway. I had other plans that I still wanted to do that day.

We got our food and paid for our bill. Then we split out of the restaurant in a hurry. On the way back to the car, I told the cabdriver to not take us to a kickback place for the rest of the time we spent in his cab that day. The cabdriver smiled and agreed, but to assure that he wasn't going to do it again, I told him I would kick his ass if he did. He must have thought I was joking because he laughed after I said it. Either that or the guy had some really good fighting skills and didn't assess me as a threat.

Everyone got in the cab, and we drove away from the restaurant, driving back through the countryside. I told the cabdriver where to take us, and he knew right where to go. Halfway through the drive, the craziest idea came over me. Now I'm not sure if anyone has told you this, but over in Thailand, if you visit one of the many pharmacies along the side of the road, you can literally get anything you want without a prescription, and I mean anything. When we first got to Thailand, we were recommended to stay away from these places, but hey, what did I care? I wanted to have a good time.

I told the cabdriver to stop at a pharmacy on the way, and both Ops and Old got a confused look on their faces so I explained myself to them. My whole plan was to stop and pick up some Viagra and really go to town on the hooker. They both laughed and asked if I really needed it. I told them no, but I'd always wanted to see if it worked as well as they say. That and I needed to pick up so condoms because I had none, and I didn't think the brothel would have any. I wasn't about ready to catch some random disease. I know what you're thinking. How can you choose to sleep with a prostitute and be worried about catching something? I guess overall that I really don't know.

We got back to the city and stopped at the first pharmacy we found. The cabdriver pulled over and parked across the street. I had to use the ATM to make sure I had enough money to buy both the pills and the prostitute but at the same time still have enough to buy drinks and party later that night. I got out of the cab, walked down the street to the nearest ATM, and pulled out the money that I needed. Right next to the ATM was a conversion chart showing the rates for money all around the world. I snapped a picture of the chart, and now I look back to this day and think to myself, "How in the hell did I manage to spend so much money in Thailand when I was getting nearly thirty dollars of their dollars to one dollar of ours?"

After I got my money, I ran across the street and went inside of the pharmacy. Now the thought that was going through my mind was either, "This is going to work, or I am going to be either dead or on my way to a Thai prison."

I approached the counter and asked the lady if she had any Viagra that I could buy. After I asked this question, she walked out from behind the counter and walked over to the front door. She turned the lock and locked us both in. Then she proceeded to pull down the shades so no one could see in or out. I was sure that I was going to die at this point.

The sweat started pouring from my heart, and my heartbeat was shooting through the roof. She walked back behind the counter and crouched down behind it. I was debating on if I should have made a run for it or if I should just wait for my fate that was most likely going to end in me being in a body bag. Once again, the paranoia factor was setting in, and the knot in my stomach was getting tighter and tighter.

She stood back up, placed a wooden box on the counter, and had to unlock it with a key. The mystery of what was in the box was slowly beginning to unravel itself, and she lifted the top of the box open and spun it around to show me what was in it. This woman had the hookup when it came to prescription drugs. She told me to take anything I wanted, and she started to ring up the price. I took a box of Viagra as I had planned on and told the lady that was going to be it. She rung me up, and the whole box cost me five dollars even. I never bought Viagra before, but I assumed that this was a good deal. I thanked the lady, and as she put away the box, I turned to the door, lifted up the shades, and unlocked the door to face the outside world of Thailand yet again.

I walked back across the street, got back into the taxi, and told both Old and Ops that it was official about the pharmacies. You can get anything you want. I then watched Ops get out of the cab and run across the street and into the pharmacy. While he was in the pharmacy, I ripped open the box and popped one of the Viagras with excitement, only wondering what waited on the road ahead of me. Old started laughing and asked if I really couldn't wait. Old then told me to have a good time and enjoy myself while it lasted.

Ops came back a few minutes later with a smile on his face. He never did share what he bought with Old and me, but whatever he bought, it sure made his day. Once we were all in the cab again, I told the driver to lie on the gas and get there as fast as he could. I mean, come on, I just popped a Viagra and didn't want the effects to go to waste. If you've ever wondered on how Viagra works, it doesn't give you an instant erection. It takes a few minutes for everything to kick in. So to answer your question, no, I did not have a rock-hard dick the whole time I was in the cab. I still have one of these pills today, even though I bought them years ago. The only reason why I haven't taken any is because I bought an off-brand version while we were in Thailand. The bad thing about the off-brand version was that it made me lose my vision for about an hour. Well, the pills got mixed up together, and now I live in fear knowing that, if I take the wrong one, I'll temporarily lose my vision.

After a short drive later, we pulled up to a big pink sign that read the words "Angel" written in yellow. I couldn't wait to get inside and find out what was waiting for me. I got out of the cab, ran to the doors, and stepped inside, and I came to find out that they weren't open yet. This had to be unreal, or someone was playing a prank on me. It was the sex capital of the world, and the damn brothel wasn't even ready to go. That's just as bad as waking up early on your day off and finding out that you have nothing to do that day.

I stepped outside back onto the street, and still determined to achieve my goal for today, I asked the cabdriver if he knew of any other places that were recommended as good as this one was. He told me to hop back into the cab, and he drove me all the way to the second-best brothel in Pattay Beach. I was praying the whole time that this one was open for many reasons. I didn't want the effects of the Viagra I just took to pass me by, and I wanted to have this done with so I could say that I slept with at least one hooker while in Thailand.

The second brothel had no sign, and I didn't even know if I were in the right place, but the cabdriver swore by it. I asked Ops and Old where they were going to be, and they pointed at a bar down the street. I told them that I would meet them there later, and I started my ascent up the stairs to the inside. I got to the top of the stairs and walked through the door, and then I saw it, the sight that let me know I had finally hit the jackpot.

I found myself standing in a lobby with a glass wall that was separating me from all of the girls who worked here. As soon as I stepped inside, all of the girls put on their best posture and started making the best sexual gestures they could at me. I was soon approached by a man wearing a button shirt and tie with the biggest smile on his face who was more than excited that I came to his store. I shook his hand and asked him how much it was going to cost me. The man told me it was going to be thirty dollars American, which came to a hundred dollars in Thai money. Now the price he told me was fair for Thailand; however, if I were in America, I would never have trusted it.

Get ready because here is another tip. Usually if a woman offers some type of special and the prices seem too good to be true, it most likely is. I have never paid anything less than $150 to sleep with a hooker, and I most likely never will because I believe you get what you pay for.

I then had to ask this question because of what just happened during the time I spent in the Philippines. I asked if the girls were here on their own free will and they weren't being forced to be here. The man then got a serious look on his face and told me that it was all their decision to do this for a living. I only trusted this man because every woman behind the glass looked as if they were in the thirties. If they were any younger, I would have questioned it. Now it came down to the hard part, choosing which one I wanted.

I felt like a kid in a candy store, taking a good look at all of them, knowing that each one most likely possessed a different unique talent. I asked the guy which one he would recommend, and he couldn't give me a straight answer, for he told me that they were all good. The one that caught my eye though, I never forgot her. All of the girls behind the glass had a number badge attached to them, so when you choose which one you wanted this way, it was easier to identify who you wanted. And there she was in the bright red, skintight dress wearing her red lipstick. Fifty-one. I never got her name, but her number was fifty-one. I'll never forget it.

I pointed her out to the man and told him that I wanted number fifty-one. He told me I made a great choice. I guess it's true. The color red does catch your eye better than any other color. The bodyguards unlocked the door to the glass room and called her number. She stood up, grabbed her purse, and made her way out of the glass room and over to me. The man then told me to follow the woman and have a good time as we walked through another door off to the side.

We entered into another room that had yet another stairwell and a set of lockers at the bottom. The lady then walked to her locker, took a key out of her purse, opened the locker, and grabbed a bucket full of stuff. Now I wasn't really sure what was exactly in the bucket, but I knew I was going to find out soon enough.

We started our climb up the stairs together as she started asking me questions about why I came to Thailand. I told her I was on vacation and looking to enjoy myself. I didn't want to tell her I was there for work because who knows what she might have asked me after that. With every step, I was getting more and more anxious to get into the room and get down to business. We only walked up three flights of stairs, but the climb initially seemed a lot longer than what it really was. I guess that's what happens when you are excited and ready to just get started already.

We reached the third floor, and there was a long corridor of doors, just like you would see at any hotel. Even two cleaning ladies were coming and going out of a room, taking out the old bedsheets and putting in the new one. This was a good sign because I knew the room would be clean and sanitized, but at the same time, I can't believe these two ladies volunteered to do this, knowing what goes on in this room. I'm sure that it's even a thought that goes through the cleaning ladies here in America as well, but I assume they choose to block this image out.

Fifty-one and I made our way down the hallway to our room, and she reached into her purse and pulled out yet another key. Not also do the ladies get their own number and locker, but they get their own keys as well. I guess it's just some of the benefits that come along with the job. Fifty-one put the key into the keyhole and opened the door to the room where all the magic would happen. I expected the room to look a little bit more eccentric than what it really was. The room looked like a normal hotel room complete with two full-sized beds and a view of the awesome building next door. I'm sure that anyone could have seen into the window and knew exactly what we were doing, but the thought never crossed my mind at the time.

Once we were in the room, Fifty-one shut the door behind her and made her way over to me as I stood in the center of the room. She set down the bucket full of stuff on the desk that was sitting against the wall, and then she turned her attention to me. She then started to take off my clothes. I told her the truth and let her know that I popped a Viagra right before I came here. I started to feel it kick in. My dick was getting rock hard, and I didn't care about hiding it anymore. Fifty-one then got a big smile on her face, and she had me completely naked.

After my clothes all hit the ground, she turned away from me, grabbed the bucket, and walked into the bathroom.

I followed her into the bathroom, but then she told me to go and sit down on the bed and wait for her. I thought she must be joking. I spent all of this time getting to this point, and I just paid for it. And now she expected me to just wait. It all better be worth it because, if not, I was going to get a refund. No, you cannot get a refund from a prostitute. That's sarcasm.

I walked back into the main room and took a seat on the bed. I turned on the TV just to have something to keep my interest until she got done doing whatever. Then I heard the sound of running water coming from the bathtub. Now I thought to myself, "You have got to be joking. She needs to take a shower before she sleeps with me. What kind of rip-off is this?" I didn't have that much time to spend here. I still had to do this and get back to Ops and Old.

I started flipping thought the channels on the TV, and I stopped to pause on the news. I couldn't make out what they were saying because they were speaking in Thai, but I could tell by the images they were showing that a storm was on the way. I kept thinking to myself that this storm wasn't going to be something that just blew over due to the fact the waves at the beach earlier were almost covering the beach. I figured, as long as the rain didn't ruin the moment I was in right at that second, what did I care?

Being lost in my own thoughts, I didn't even realize that the water from the bathtub stopped running. Fifty-one walked back out into the main room where I was, and she started to take off her clothes right in front of me. I knew it was about to get good. First, she took off her shoes, and then she slid out of the skintight dress she was wearing and threw it on the opposite bed that I was sitting on. She then took off her bra and panties and had me follow her into the bathroom. Right then, I saw what the bucket was used for. Bath items filled it.

The bathroom didn't look anything special. In fact, it looked like just an ordinary bathroom that you would find in a home neighborhood. It had the white tile walls, the white toilet, and even the white bathtub. The only thing missing from this bathroom was a shower curtain. Apparently, they don't believe in shower curtains in Thai brothels. Bubbles filled the bathtub, and there was even a scented candle she lit that was sitting on the back of the toilet. The only thing was that Fifty-one left the bright lights on, so if she were going for a romantic setting, she never achieved it.

She asked me to get into the bathtub and get comfortable, and she climbed in after me. She placed her legs on the side of mine, sat with her back against the wall, and faced me. She had me then lean back into the warm water and enjoy myself. Once Fifty-one and I were settled into the tub, she then grabbed my dick and started going to town. That's right. I started getting a hand job while I was in a bathtub full of bubble bath. Now I can't tell if it were the bubbles that made my dick so insensitive to her touch, if it were the pills, or if it were the fact that I masturbate too much. Because of this fact, it took my forever to cum, but at least I got to relax in a nice hot tub for once.

This hand job was taking so long that I was getting so used to the warm water that I started to regret taking the pills after the water started to cool down. I had to help speed this up so I pulled her forward, got as close as I could, and started making out with her and sucking on her tits, all while trying to make sure she could still get enough movement with her hand. The craziest part about all of this was that she never once ruined her makeup. It remained flawless the whole time she was in the water. Her red lips looked so good the whole time though. I'm not quite sure what it is about red lipstick, but it is a memorizing factor that can attract any man even though it's usually related to being a trashy color. Maybe that's the reason why it works so well.

We must have spent close to a half hour in that bathtub before I felt anything at all, and all I could think about was how badly I wanted to explode. Once the feeling got close, I let her go and lay back into the tub. I was finally feeling it until I came, shooting my load right into the bathwater. Fifty-one then squeezed all she could out of my dick, and then she let go and leaned back herself. I had to take a minute to myself to let my energy catch back up to me. I can say that, for never taking Viagra before, it sure made the feeling of cumming a lot more sensual.

After a few minutes of relaxing, Fifty-one reached behind her and pulled the plug out to the bathtub, and the water started to drain. We both stood up, but she insisted I stay in the tub. Fifty-one then turned on the shower and cleaned me off. So not only did I get a bath and hand job, I got a shower and scrubbed down by another woman. That was a win in my book. At least I wouldn't be leaving smelling like Thai hooker. Fifty-one scrubbed me down and then turned off the water, grabbed a towel she had sitting on top of the toilet lid, and dried me off. I swear this treatment just kept getting better. It was like I was being treated like a king.

The towel dry was over, and she had me get out of the tub and head back into the main room. I sat back down on the bed and waited for Fifty-one to come out. I turned off the TV and grabbed my clothes to put them back on. Before I could even put my clothes back on, Fifty-one came out of the bathroom, grabbed my clothes from me, and put them back down. I guess this was her way of saying that I wasn't over yet. Fifty-one then turned to her purse and pulled out a pack of cigarettes. Now I don't smoke, and I did not intend to start as she offered me to smoke with her. When I declined, she acted as if she just committed a crime. I told her, if she were to smoke, I wouldn't have a problem with it.

She took a cigarette out of the pack and put the rest of the pack back into her purse. She then opened the drawer to the desk, grabbed a book of matches from inside the desk, and lit her cigarette. This got me thinking about what else were in the drawers of this room. I checked both the desk and the nightstand in between the two beds and of course found nothing more than just the typical room Bible. Go figure.

Fifty-one made her way over to the window, and I soon followed. She opened the window to let out the smoke, and we engaged in a conversation about what her life was like in Thailand. Fifty-one was not married. No, she did not have any kids. She said she used to work in one of the go-go bars in Jomtien Beach, but it wasn't enough to support herself, so she changed workplaces. Now at the go-go bars, you can even take a woman home from there, but from what I hear, this doesn't happen as much because of all the competition between the other girls and a lot of tourists don't know this right away. Fifty-one then looked to the sky and told me that there was a storm on the way and that, if it got to rain too bad, I should find shelter wherever I was.

Not long after our conversation, Fifty-one's cigarette was getting down to the end. She then flipped the cigarette out the window and closed it. I then asked if she were any good at giving massages, and she instructed that I lay down on the bed. She sucked at giving massage. All she did was rub my legs and do a few compressing movements until I got bored and decided it was time for round two.

I looked at her and said, "Let's have sex."

Fifty-one then got a big smile on her face. She hopped off the bed in pure excitement as she quickly got to her purse to grab a condom and get back onto the bed, almost as if time stood still, and she really never left my side.

Fifty-one leaped back onto the bed, and I pulled her in close to me and started kissing her. I then rolled us over, and I got on top of her. Fifty-one started struggling, trying to get the condom unwrapped because of all the movement that was going on. I kept telling her to just forget about it because I was ready to get it on, but then I remembered that it would be in my best interest and for better health if I wore it. I let go of Fifty-one and sat back on my knee on the bed. Now the cool thing about prostitutes is they have a unique way of putting on condoms if I haven't explained this before. Honestly, I believe this is in the prostitute handbook somewhere in the world. The whole process goes down something like this:

Step 1: Open condom and remove from package.

Step 2: Put condom on tip of penis.

Step 3: Unroll condom until it is past the head.

Step 4: Proceed to unroll condom using only your mouth.

Step 5: After condom is unrolled to base, proceed to warm up penis with a blow job.

I believe this is written down somewhere, and if it isn't, well it is now. And I believe that every prostitute should do this. It creates for a really good opener to the sexual encounter and gets the receiver relaxed. After all, most people don't sleep with prostitutes, so why not make a good first impression? It might change someone's mind. This is the exact way that Fifty-one put the condom on me, just as most of the other girls had done before and did after her as well.

Usually, I would let her continue on with the blow job for a little longer, but considering the fact that I was still getting the full effect from the Viagra that I took earlier, I cut her off and got right to the sex. I pushed Fifty-one back onto the bed, threw her legs over my shoulders, and went to town. Fifty-one happened to be very flexible, and at some point, I actually had her pinned up against the headboard of the bed with her ankles behind her head, making her look like a human pretzel. My God, never in my life had anyone fucked so good.

Now I wasn't sure if it were the Viagra that I took that made it feel like forever or if it were the fact she already made me cum once just a few short minutes ago. Hell, it could even be the fact that I masturbate so much that made it seem like this sex was never going to end. Now I enjoy lasting for a long time. After all, it's every guy's dream to fuck forever, but trust me. Lasting forever isn't all it is talked up to be. People get tired, and being a guy, you're usually doing all of the work. Ladies, help a guy out from time to time and get more involved.

I started to wonder if I paid for the room with the original cost because my thoughts of having to spend the night seemed like they were becoming a reality. Just when it started to seem like it was going to take all night, a miracle must have happened. Cumming never felt so good because I knew I could finally take a break. I let go of Fifty-one and rolled over onto the bed. The next few minutes felt like they flew by as both Fifty-one and I tried to get our energy back into us.

It didn't take long for Fifty-one to recoup and get off the bed. She walked right back into the bathroom and turned on the water. The only thought that was going through my head was, "I can't do it again this soon."

I started to drift in and out as I was getting to the point where I could have fallen asleep with no problem. The sound of running water was still in the background as I was brought out of my haze by Fifty-one standing over me and telling me to get out of bed. I knew I wouldn't have the energy to make it a whole round, but I pulled myself together and got out of bed. I walked into the bathroom to see that Fifty-one had left the shower running. This, to me, was a sign of relief because I knew that all I would be getting was another scrub down. Fifty-one and I both stepped into the shower, and she proceeded to wash me down yet again. I can see why they give a person a shower. Now I'm not going to lie. I can understand that no one should leave a place smelling like sex, but at the time, I didn't care. In fact, I was more so impressed because I thought it was funny.

Fifty-one washed me down, and the shower was over before I even noticed it. Fifty-one handed me a towel and told me to dry off and wait for her out in the main room. Now what I did next now seems unmoral, and I should have never done it. But at the time when you are in a got-to-go situation, you make it happen. I walked back out to the main room, and the feeling of having to piss overtook me. I could have easily walked back into the bathroom and pissed in the toilet, but I felt that pissing in front of a prostitute or yet any woman you hardly know is a messed-up thing to do. So my creative juices started flowing.

I started looking at everything that could hold my piss that I could hide it in. I thought about pissing on the bed and hiding it with the blanket over top. I thought about pissing out the window. I even thought about pissing in the corner and hoping she wouldn't notice. Finally, my plans ended when I saw the trash can.

Now I'll let you know that the whole time, Fifty-one was in her bathroom, cleaning the tub and the floor, getting it ready for the next people who might use the room. My genius idea came when I decided to grab the trash can by the desk.

I took the trash can over to the corner with me and unloaded my full bladder right into it. Halfway through my piss, I started thinking again about how I was going to hide the smell so Fifty-one wouldn't notice. I pushed out my piss as fast as I could and set down the trash can in the corner. I must have filled the trash can between a quarter to halfway full. I quickly searched the room for something I could put in the trash can to help cover the smell. Once again, my creative juices started flowing to my brain, and I grabbed one of the pillows off the bed that we didn't have sex on. I took the pillow and shoved it right in the trash can.

Now, I know I shouldn't have done any of this, and I felt bad for the cleaning lady who had to deal with this. The bigger thought going through my head was that the cleaning lady was most likely going to think that I was into some weird piss fetish. I'm not going to lie. If the cleaning lady reported it to the boss, they most likely would have assumed that Fifty-one had some weird fetish she was hiding, too. I guess, if you're going to do something you shouldn't be doing in the first place, you might as well go out with a bang.

I sat around on the edge of the bed we had sex on and waited for Fifty-one to come out of the bathroom. I knew I was done and had to get the hell out of there. Besides, Ops and Old were down the street waiting for me, and we still had other things that we wanted to accomplish that day. Fifty-one came out of the bathroom, looked at me, and smiled. She then started to reach for her pack of cigarettes as I told her I had to leave. Fifty-one got a look of confusion on her face and asked me why. I told her that I had a few buddies waiting for me down the street at the bar. Fifty-one put her cigarettes back and handed me my clothes.

One thing I've realized is that, not only with prostitutes but even with everyone in the world, when it comes down to sex, we'll help each other take our clothes off, but once it's over, no one helps you put your clothes back on. It's a sad world we live in.

Fifty-one and I got our clothes back on, and I looked around the room to make sure that I wasn't forgetting anything and to make sure that the trash can full of piss hadn't spilled over. Fifty-one gathered everything that she had in the bucket she brought with her, and we left the room. The cleaning lady was right down the hall, and I knew it wouldn't take long for her to start cleaning the room I was just in. It still amazes me that someone would choose to do this for a living, knowing full well what goes on in every room. You have to give credit where credit is needed, so here's to you cleaning ladies. I appreciate the things you do.

We reached the end of the hallway and made our way down the stairs. Once we got to the bottom, Fifty-one walked back to the locker and put the bucket back. She closed the locker, and we made our way back out into the main room. The same man who greeted me was there and asked how my time was and why I was leaving so soon. I told him that I had to catch back up with my buddies who had been waiting for me. The man smiled and thanked me for coming by as I watched Fifty-one go back into the room behind the glass window. It's crazy to think that things such as glass can be used to create a barrier, but yet you can see the whole world outside. I guess it takes a strong person to go to work and sit behind a glass window that almost acts like a prison every day. I hope that, whatever Fifty-one is doing with her life currently, she's happy doing it.

I walked out of the building very casually, and I started running as soon as I got outside. I made a beeline down the street until I reached the bar where Ops and Old were at. I'm sure that everyone on the street looking at me was probably thinking that I was being chased by some bad people. And trust me, if they found out that I had just pissed in their trash can, they probably would be chasing after me. I kept running and ran right into the bar, right to the table where Ops and Old were sitting. They both looked at me with a confused look on their faces and asked the same question.

"Why are you running?"

I responded very calmly and said, "I just pissed in a trash can."

I got the exact responses that I thought I would get. Ops laughed and told me how funny he thought it was that I went to a whorehouse to piss in a trash can. Old, on the other hand, didn't find it so funny and asked me what kind of fucked-up things that Fifty-one and I were into. I explained the story about how I had no other options and I would appreciate it if we got the hell out of the area fast. Old, on the other hand, thought it would be more humorous to him if he drank his Red Label and Coke as slow as he could. Old was just waiting to see if anyone would come looking for me. The best part was that no one ever came. I guess the cleaning lady was so used to it that nothing phased her at this point.

Old finally finished his drink, and we walked out of the bar. I turned out that the cabdriver sat in the car the whole time and waited for us. I did understand that we paid the man already, but you think he would have went to the bar himself or gotten something to eat. I guess, just like the cleaning lady, he's so used to waiting that it didn't faze him anymore.

We all got back into the cab, and the cabdriver smiled at me and asked how everything was. I guess it's very common after you get done sleeping with a prostitute to be asked how it was. I told the cabdriver that it was great and thanked him for showing me the place.

After my short conversation with the cabdriver, it was time to figure out what to do next. I had already gotten my fill for the day and figured it was up to someone else to decide where we should go. I guess I should say that Ops was easily amused by anything that was shiny or exploded. I like to think that he enjoyed the simple things in life. Ops suggested we get fireworks and blow up a beach. Old and I were down for whatever at this point, so we agreed. The cabdriver stepped off the brakes and got us back on the road again.

I wish I could say I did a lot of sightseeing in Thailand while we were driving around, but everything looked the same. The buildings were built high like skyscrapers, children played out in the street, and most places didn't even have any doors or windows. The whole city looked like one giant open market. The arrival at the firework store really amazed me because it blended in so well that you wouldn't know it was there unless someone showed you it.

Once again, it seemed like things would be getting shady. Ops flew out of the car due to his attraction to explosions. Old and I followed in shortly after, but from what I saw, this didn't look like any ordinary fireworks store.

The store was actually ran by an old Chinese couple that had half of their store set up with Asian antiques and the other half of the store set up with Chinese fireworks. I found this to be odd due to the fact that, if the fireworks went off, the whole store would be destroyed, ruining thousands, if not millions of dollars, invested in antiques. The other part that blew me away was, if you're in a country that makes fireworks, why would they have to import fireworks from a neighboring country?

The whole time I was browsing around the store, I couldn't help but notice that Ops was trying to buy the whole store. I swear Ops bought enough fireworks to make the Fourth of July look like a warm-up party. Once Ops paid for the fireworks, it was a matter of transporting them to where we needed to go. So we decided that we would put all the fireworks into the truck. I'm not going to lie. If we got pulled over, I'm sure the cops would have thrown us in jail for looking like we were trying to commit an act of terrorism.

I guess I should warn you that this wasn't the worst thing that Ops bought. He happened to be a big gun collector, and you couldn't open a door or sit in a chair in his house without being in arm's reach of a gun. Once during this time period, we were in India, and he bought a live duck from a convenience store. The guy once spent every night for a week straight observing a boat yard because he wanted to swim onto a boat and take a piss on the bow of a random boat. He also took boxes of Pop Tarts, handed them out to random people on the street, and took pictures of people holding them. Yeah, Ops had some adventure in him, but he was completely unpredictable.

Back into the cab yet again on our way to the beach, I could see all of the excitement on Spec's face like a kid on Christmas morning. The drive to the beach didn't take long. The beach that we went to was actually located shortly outside of the city, but there was a restaurant on the beach we were about to blow up. As we pulled up to the beach, it started setting in my mind about how long it would be until the owners of the restaurant called the cops on us. They never did, which is one of the cool things about Thailand. You can literally do just about anything you want.

I didn't know how the loud noises were going to be with the amount of energy I already drained, so I figured it would be a good time to started drinking. As Spec got set up with the fireworks, Old and I decided that we would walk over to the restaurant and see if they would sell us beer. We were in luck because they didn't even give us a reason why they couldn't sell it to us. They just handed it over like it was a common thing. Not shortly after being handed my beer, the loud sounds of fireworks were going off. The lady behind the counter asked us what the noise was. We told her that we had a friend who liked shiny and explosive stuff.

Old and I stepped back outside the restaurant, and we saw Ops lighting off fireworks and throwing them faster than they were made. If we only had old WWII uniforms, I'm pretty sure we could have reenacted the invasion of Normandy Beach. After a while, the employees and even the diners at the restaurant came out to watch the amazing firework show that Spec was putting on. We even were able to capture the attention of random people who were passing by. One good thing I took away from this was that Ops would always have a job in Thailand as a fireworks performer.

The fireworks show was ending, and I was running low on beer. I ran back over to the restaurant and got a beer to go. I made it back outside just in time to watch the last few fireworks being blown off. After it was all said and done and the smoke cleared, sand was blown all over the place, and the beach was reduced to a crater. It was crazy to think that most of the day by this point was spent by eating food, sleeping with a prostitute, and blowing up a beach. The only thing left to do for the day was get drunk. Besides by this time, the dark clouds were rolling in, and a storm was coming.

It was back in the cab for one last drive to where we got picked up. The cabdriver dropped us off. We said thanks for driving us around all day, and we parted to go our separate ways. We had picked a bad time to get out of the cab because, once the cabdriver pulled away, the downpour started right away. We ran around the corner to the closest bar, and sure enough, it happened to be the one bar where our supervisors were. Yes, even over in another country, being in the same place as your supervisor still sucks, even if they are the only people who speak English besides you.

As soon as we stepped in the door, they noticed us right away and offered for us to sit with them. I hate when this happens because you don't want to sit with them, but yet, if you don't, you look like a complete asshole. The one way I found to get out of this was to sit at a table close to them but far enough away where you don't have to talk to them. To my surprise, our supervisors even bought us our first round. I just wished I could have enjoyed my beer more.

All three of us drank our beers as fast as we could so we could get the hell out of there and away from the people we worked for. I will admit that it was pretty funny watching most of these married men let themselves go by getting drunk, acting stupid, and letting some random girl hang all over them while their wives weren't around. I wished I had gotten pictures.

The beers were finally gone, and we were all in a hurry to get out of there. At this point, we didn't even care if we got soaked from the rain. We just wanted to be someone that our bosses weren't. We thanked our bosses for the round, and we left. Old, Ops, and I made a few trips though some back alleys and ended up at the same bar that Ops and Old were at the night before. A few other people we worked with were here.

As we took our seat at the bar, Old got this uneasy look on his face as if he didn't want to be here. I asked Old if everything were all right, and all he did was sit there with the same look on his face. I looked around to see what was bothering him, and sure enough, the bartender was giving him some weird looks from across the bar. The bartender was a short, petite man with a flamboyant look to him. You could tell that the man was gay from a mile away. I had to find out what the real story was, and since Old wasn't talking, I had to ask Ops what happened.

He told me that the night before, while Old and Ops were at the bar, the bartender kept taking pictures of him with Old. Old didn't think anything of it. He thought the bartender was just a nice, friendly guy. It didn't take long for the bartender to show his friendly side to Old.

The man ended up sneaking up behind Old and giving him a big kiss on the cheek and snapped a picture of it. Now, I'll remind you that Old is married and he's not gay, so this creeped out Old quite a bit. It got better because, after the picture was taken, the bartender ran down to the street to a store to get the pictures developed.

About an hour later, the bartender came back, found Old, and handed him the doubles that he had made.

Now, Old didn't exactly know what to do with his pictures. He just knew that he was going to get rid of them and make sure no one ever saw him. The bartender, on the other hand, had posted the pictures up in the bar for everyone to see, and I'm sure that there still there to this day.

Back to present day now, I couldn't help but laugh at Old for everything I had just heard. The typical response came out of Old's mouth that would come out of any guy's mouth really, telling me to shut up and saying it wasn't funny. I told Old that it was all water under the bridge and he could stop freaking out at any time. Old then proceeded to tell me that the photos he was given got misplaced on the bus and he didn't know where they were. It turned out that Old had taken a nap on the bus last night and dropped the pictures. When he woke up, he forgot all about them. After the last bus ride back the night before, the supervisors checked the bus to make sure nothing was left behind. Sure enough, they found the pictures and questioned Old a few days after we left Thailand about the pictures.

Needless to say, we didn't stay at this bar much longer either. We all ordered a round and tried to enjoy what we could out of the beer we had. This night seemed like it was turning out bad because we couldn't find a bar worth staying at. The bartender kept creeping out Old by staring at him the whole time, making the whole situation uncomfortable for everyone. I figured I would break the tension, take all of the attention of the bartender off Old, and turn it on myself. I wouldn't normally do this for most people, but I could see how bad it was bothering Old. I set down my beer and told Ops and Old that I would be right back.

I walked right up to the bartender, gave him a hug, and yelled in the bar, "I love you, man!" I let go of him and made my way back to my seat.

I got back to the table, and it was the same thing as before. Ops was laughing his ass off, and Old had a confused look on his face. I felt I could sit there and explain I took the attention off Old, but I figured this time that I would just let them think whatever they wanted to think. I grabbed my beer and finished what was left in it, and we all made our way out of the bar. The search for a good bar was still our top priority, and this search wasn't ending anytime soon.

We first decided that it would be a good idea to let Ops lead us to a bar, but instead, he led us into some random hotel that happened to be smack dab right in the middle of Jomtien. Old and I questioned where Ops was taking us, and he said it was a shortcut. I would like to know how Ops thought this was a shortcut because he had never been to Jomtien before, but I'll let you know he has led us into other situations before where he's claimed that it was a shortcut.

After following Ops around for the past hour and ending up in a laundry room, a kitchen, and electrical room, we decided to give up on Ops taking us anywhere. Old was up next to lead us to a good bar where we wouldn't have to leave. At least this was what we thought would happen. Now if I didn't think that the pictures in the bar and the bartender were bad before, I was wrong. Old led us down a street that had all kinds of flashing lights and loud music coming out of every building. I figured that we would sure find a good bar on this street, but after taking a closer look, I knew this wasn't going to happen.

The three of us walked all the way down the street until we realized where we were. Out of all the streets in Jomtien, Old happened to lead us down the one and only street that was made up of nothing but gay bars. This street couldn't have been more obvious that it was the gay bar street due to that fact that penis statues were in front of every bar and men were making out with each other on the front steps of every bar. I knew we had to get the hell out of there.

The three of us bolted down the street and got back onto the main road. Once back on the main road, we all stopped running and recouped back together. Spec and I both looked at Old and asked him if he wanted to tell us something. I mean, I knew the guy was married and you could do anything you wanted in Thailand, and so far, Old was really living up to the opportunity. Old just looked at us and said that he didn't know. To this day, I don't know what he was thinking when he led us down that street in Thailand, but I am sure to be cautious if he ever led me anywhere again.

Ops and I took everything that just happened for what it was worth. We continued our adventure to find a bar on the next street over. The good thing about this street was that it wasn't full of gay bars, but yet the odd thing about this street was that most of the bars were located right in the middle of the street. The bars that weren't had no doors or windows. It was just one giant open area. Out of all the bars we chose to go to on this street, we walked into the only Irish bar. Yes, I understand that we were in Thailand and we chose to go to an Irish bar.

We took our seats at the corner of the bar and ordered our drinks. The bartender was a short, stocky man with no hair and pale skin. Being an immigrant from Ireland, he was interested in knowing where we were from. After all, we didn't blend in with all of the locals. I wished that he had never asked this question. Ops decided that he wanted to tell the bartender that he was from Canada, and Old told the bartender that he was from Oregon. I figured I would go along with their idea, and I told the bartender I was from Mexico. The Irish bartender laughed, told us welcome to Thailand, and walked away to help the rest of the bar.

I asked Ops why he got the idea to tell the bartender that he was from Canada. After all, Ops is originally from New Hampshire, and he always has to let people know about it. On the other hand, Ops worked and currently lived in Oregon with the rest of us. Ops proceeded to tell Old and me that, when he told people he was from the United States, some people reacted negative against it, but when he told people he was from Canada, everybody loved him. He did have a point. I mean, how many times have the Canadians done anything wrong?

Not long after Ops got done explaining himself, a woman who worked in the bar as well came walking over to us. She was originally from Thailand with long black hair and a petite body. She asked us the same questions about where we were from, so we gave her the same response as the man before. Ops then asked her what her story was and how she got a job at an Irish bar. She proceeded to tell us that he husband owned the bar and she was originally from Thailand. The thing that came out of her mouth blew me away. She told us that she had been married to her husband for about five years now and she had two more years left with him before she left him.

I kept thinking to myself, "This is a hard thing to deal with. I hope he knows what's coming to him." I asked the lady why she planned to leave her husband. I guess the lady had a rule that she would get married, but after seven years of marriage, she would leave him because she wanted something new in life. I thought that this was an interesting way. You live life building a relationship with someone, only to find out that, after being married for seven years, you want nothing to do with him or her anymore. I guess I really can't talk because, at the time, what I was doing wasn't much better.

The lady got done telling us her story, and I heard Ops come out with it and say that Old and he were married. I looked at Ops, and he told the lady that they had been married for several years now. And because of where they lived and their jobs, they didn't get to see each other all the time. The lady got a sad look on her face and told the two of them that she was happy they got to go on vacation to Thailand together. Now, this was when things get odd. Old told the lady that, because of the separation, they brought me from Mexico to use as a sex slave. I would love to know where they came up with these ideas.

It was amazing to think all of the things that could happen in twenty-four hours. I went from being a guy who was blacked out to sleeping with a prostitute, and then now, I was reduced to being a Mexican sex slave for two people who weren't even married. I guess you could say that life was good. The lady asked Ops and Old what they did with me exactly, and they both replied by saying, "Whatever we want to do to him."

Old had to make an example of this and told me to start eating the paper towel that was sitting at the end of the bar. I gave Old the look of "You have got to be shitting me!" I went for it and grabbed the paper towel roll. I ripped off a sheet of paper towel and went to town on it. Ops proceeded to tell the lady that the main reason they brought me from Mexico was that, because they couldn't be with each other all of the time, they could use me to have sex with and send back and forth to each other. They explained it as having a mutual third party in the relationship without having to cheat on each other.

I'm not going to lie. They were both pretty creative and great at thinking fast.

The night was ending, and we had to get back soon to catch the last bus back. We finished our drinks at the bar and started our route back to the hotel where the bus dropped us off. As soon as we got back, we walked into the office to check in with or supervisors, and sure enough, the same ones who were working were the same ones who were just at the bar a few short hours ago. I asked them if they were okay to be working right now, and the only response I got was to shut the hell up and mind my own business. I took that as a, "No, I'm drunk and not responsible at this time right now."

The three of us checked back in and got on the bus. I took my seat in one of the back rows. Shortly after, more people started piling on the bus, and one of these people happened to be a drunk Swamp. I wasn't really sure what he did with his day, but whatever he did, it looked like he had a good time. Swamp took a seat next to me and let me know that he was happy to see me and he hoped I was enjoying Thailand. Swamp then took a laptop out of his backpack that he carried all day. He took the memory chip out of his camera and plugged it into his laptop so he could upload his images. Swamp then turned on his music, handed me his headphones and his laptop, and told me to watch them. Swamp got up out of his seat and walked off the bus. I put the headphones into my ears, put my head against the window, and slowly fell asleep.

One of my supervisors woke me up about an hour later. I took the headphones out of my ears to hear the news about why we hadn't left yet. The storm from earlier caused some damage along the way, and they wouldn't be able to get any out to fix it until the next day. They told everyone that they were going to allow us to spend the night in Jomtien. This was working out in my favor because I already had plans to spend the night in Jomtien the next day. Two nights in the city started sounding like a dream come true. They had us find someone to share a room with and report back to them as soon as we had our roommate and room number.

Everyone scurried to find someone to room with as if it were a decision that would affect the rest of their lives. I looked around for Ops and Old, but both of them had to be up early the next day to head back, so that option was out. I looked for Swamp; however, I couldn't find him anywhere. Word, another guy I worked with, approached me. Word stands about five-foot-seven with a combover haircut and a creeper mustache in the making.

Word had just started working with us a few months back, so we didn't really know too much about him, but for whatever else, he told me he got along good with everyone, at least for a little while that. Since I didn't have any other options, I figured I would go for it.

The two of us made our way to the front desk of the hotel and split the cost on the room. I can't believe that I spent fifty dollars American on a five-star hotel. God, I love Thailand, and I love that exchange rate, too. Word and I both got our copies of the room keys and made our way back to our supervisors to check in with them. We gave them our room information and started our walk to our room when I heard the loud sounds of yelling in the backroom. They had finally discovered Swamp. After Swamp got off the bus, he went and sat down in the courtyard. And he waited until it was the last call to get back on the bus. Since last call to get back on the bus was taking forever, Swamp decided that he would leave with a few other people to the closest store to grab more beer.

Swamp and the others came back with the beer they bought and proceeded to drink in the courtyard. This already upset our supervisor because he left the hotel after he had already checked in. They were considering that something could have happened to him. They never took the beer away from Swamp originally. They continued to let him drink, and they were going to let him take it on the bus with him. Swamp continued to drink his beer, and instead of getting on the bus, he went to the bathroom instead. When our boss found him, Swamp was passed out on the toilet completely naked with an empty beer bottle on the floor. I guess you could say that Thailand has that effect on people.

I'm not sure what they did to Swamp after that. I do know that it was one of those moments that don't happen all of the time. The yelling in the background happened for quite some time, but it faded out as I got closer to my room. Once inside of my room, I climbed right onto one of the beds and fell asleep, waiting for the next day to come and see what adventures Thailand had in store for me.

I woke up the next morning, being able to still remember everything from the night before. I couldn't wait to get back out and see what else Thailand had to offer me with only having one full day left to do anything. I was supposed to be meeting Spark and Dick later in the day because we had plans to hit all of the bars at night and spend the night in Jomtien. Due to the damage from the storm before, I realized it would be a minute until I met with them.

Word was still asleep when I woke up so I figured I would hop in the shower. They recommended that we didn't drink any of the water out of the sink while we were in these other countries due to poor plumbing and bacteria in the water. I sure hoped it was safe to take a shower in. Nothing bad happened to me, so I suppose everything went well. I took my shower, and by the time I got out of the bathroom, Word was awake, and I asked if he were ready to start his day. Having no hesitation at all, he jumped out of bed because he needed to go shopping for a SIM card so he could call his girlfriend back home. I don't really understand how so many relationships stay so strong with so much differences between the two people, but hey, more power to the people that can make it work out.

Word and I gathered all of our things, left the room, and headed for the front desk. We checked out of our room and returned the hotel keys. I do have to admit that the hotel was nice, and if I ever go back to Jomtien, it will most likely be the same hotel I stayed in. The location is great. It's close to all of the bars and water. If you're ever in Jomtien, Thailand, stay at the Jomtien resort. After checking out of the room, we had to check in with our supervisors to let them know we were still alive and leaving the hotel.

I guess I should have known who was checking people in and out in the morning. It was the same two people from before. I don't think these people even slept. They probably just hung out at the bars all night, got really drunk, and went right back to work, only to go back to the bars when they got off again. We checked in with the two of them, and I let them know I'd be back later to meet up with Spark and Dick.

Word and I started on the adventure on the day that lay ahead of us. The first thing that was on my mind was to get some food in me. I didn't really care what I ate, just as long as it was something. We started walking down a random road in the city, and I saw a cart that was parked over on the side of the road. A Thai man had flagged down this cart earlier to get some food from it. Another cool thing about Thailand is that they have these carts that people ride around all of the city. They look like bicycles with grills of deep fryers attached to them. Anytime you want something to eat off these carts, all you have to do is wave them down.

Word and I approached the cart to see what they were selling. The locals couldn't stop raving about what they had, so I had to try some of it. I handed the guy fifty cents, and he handed me a bag of what looked like rolls and a cup full of icing. I had no idea what I ate, but

I do know that it tasted like donuts and it was amazing. I couldn't get enough of it so I went through two more bags before I even left the cart. I kept trying to find that same cart to get more of it the rest of the time I was in Thailand, but I never could find it. I waved down every cart I could, but they all failed to have what I wanted.

After walking away from the cart, it was time to find Word's SIM card. We started off by having no luck, but we got stopped by every cabdriver in the world trying to drive us around everywhere. Now I can't say that I wouldn't have liked having a cabdriver drive me around all day, but I was supposed to be meeting two people later. After walking around the city and not quite knowing where we were, we both decided that we should head back to the bar district. We most likely would have had more luck there.

We started walking through some random side streets, and we came to a dead end. Sometimes walking into dead ends can lead to an adventure of a lifetime. One of the doors at the very end of this street had screams of pain and agony coming from it, and I wanted to see what was going on. I know what you're thinking. Why would anyone walk into the sounds of screaming? I told Word that we should check it out, and he didn't even have a care in the world. He wanted to check it out with me.

We walked up to the door and looked inside, and we found ourselves looking at a Thai boxing fight. If you've ever seen Thai boxing on TV, it's the real deal. These people were getting messed up. Blood was going everywhere, and people were being knocked out, one after another. I couldn't think of a better way to start my day then with donuts and violence. We stood in the doorway for a while before a big Thai man approached us. He didn't seem so happy that we were standing there. He had a shaved head, a pissed-off look on his face, and an arm that he turned into a sleeve of tattoos. Now I thought that we were in a bad place.

I explained to the man that we were lost and had stopped in to see what was going on. The man proceeded to tell us that outsiders weren't welcome to training. I thought to myself, "If this is just training, I can't wait to see what the real deal is." I can't say I know many trainings where they go all out and try to kill their sparring partner, but I was into it.

I asked the man when the fight would be, and he handed me a flyer. The fight was set for two days from now, and the only thought in my head was that I was going to have to miss someone most likely dying because of the way these guys fought. That's a good way to kill a fun time.

I took the flyer and said thank you to the man. I was so upset from it that I threw the flyer in the first trash can I saw. I figured, if I couldn't see the real thing, I didn't want something to remind me of missing it.

Word and I started our adventure of walking around again. Now what happened next isn't something I went looking for, but I heard that it's very common in Thailand. I wanted to get a Thai massage so I could say that I experienced it. Yes, many places in Thailand use the whole massage therapy thing as a front. That was not what I was looking for; however, I wanted an actual Thai massage.

Because of others using it as a front, it's very hard to find a place that actually gave real Thai massages so I figured I would give any random one a try and see if they offered a real massage. I was in. If not, then I knew where I was. Word and I kept walking when we found a place just outside of the bar district. I'm not sure if all of the places are connected, but they had a dress code at every massage place in Jomtien. By this, I mean that, at every massage place in Thailand, every girl who worked in Jomtien at a massage place wore the same thing, and I mean every girl. This day, it happened to be a red top with blue jeans.

Word and I reached the front door of the massage place, and a girl sitting outside warmly welcomed us both. That's another thing they do. They all sit outside of the massage places and try to pull inside random tourists from off the street. She didn't have to worry because it didn't take much convincing to get me in the door. The store must have just opened because some of the girls were still getting ready. The lady from the front led me to what I would like to call a room, but really, it was just a mattress on the ground with a few sheets thrown over it. The room was very poorly lit, but I had nothing to fear at this point. If anything happened, hey, it was going to happen. She told me to wait there and said the girl giving me a massage would be right over.

The lady then took Word over to another room and pulled a sheet to close off the room I was in. I started to feel like I was more in a shady hospital about to get my kidney taken out. I lay down on the mattress, and a few short minutes later, a girl pulled back the sheet and walked into the room. She was a little bit of a thicker girl with long dark hair and beautiful dark eyes. For the rest of this story, we'll call her Thick. Thick smiled at me and told me to take off my clothes and lay facedown on the mattress. I proceeded to follow her instructions and waited for the massage to begin.

If you've ever had a Thai massage before, then you know exactly what it is. If not, I'll explain it to you. It is a type of massage that consists of mostly stretching and compression moves. It's designed to more so help stretch out the body and make it more flexible than it is to relax the body. I'm not going to lie. If you don't have anything wrong with your body medically, I recommend to give a Thai massage a try. You'll enjoy it.

Thick took me through every Thai move she could think of, stretching my body in ways I never knew my body could stretch. Before I knew it, the massage was over. It's crazy to think a massage could last only an hour, yet they always seem like they last longer than that.

After the massage, I laid on the mattress for a minute to get out of my relaxed state so I could get up. Just before I had time to get up, it happened. Thick climbed on top of me and asked me if I wanted to fuck. I thought to myself, "How could I pass this up?" I mean, I knew I shouldn't do it, but hey, if she were offering, I wasn't complaining. Thick then leaned back and smiled at me again.

I shook my head and told her, "Yeah, let's do it."

Thick told me it would be thirty dollars American. Thick then stood up and left the room to get a condom.

I'm not going to lie. I'm really glad the prostitutes come prepared. It makes my job easier. All I have to do is show up then. If you ever do decide to sleep with a prostitute, don't forget to bring your own just in case she doesn't have any.

Thick was away, and I reached over for my shorts that I was wearing that day to get my wallet. I pulled thirty dollars out of my wallet and laid there, waiting for Thick to come back. I laid there on the mattress, thinking, "I hope Word doesn't mind. This is going to take a while." But like I said, I didn't know much about the kid, and I was going for it, whether he liked it or not. Thick came back through the sheet with a condom in her hand, smiled at me, and asked if I were ready.

I smiled and said, "Let's do this."

Thick kneeled down next to me, and sure enough, it started it off as the same routine. Remember the blow job technique that I told you guys about earlier. Yeah, that was exactly what she did. The only difference was that I didn't pop a Viagra beforehand this time. The blow job ended, and Thick had me get off the mattress and get on top of her. The way sex usually starts with a prostitute is they all want to be in a missionary position, just like mostly every girl wants it to start. The difference between prostitutes and girls you might pick up from the bar is that prostitutes are willing to try just about any position known to many. After all, you're paying for it, so it's the way services should be rendered. Most women you pick up from the bar, however, usually never move away from missionary position, and it gets old really quick.

As I said, it started out in missionary position and then moved to doggie, and last was cowgirl. Now for the room being so small, I was surprised we were able to move around as much as we did, but we made it work out for us. To end it all, Thick did something that no other girls have done before her. She got off my dick and proceeded to take the condom off me. She finished me off by going back to giving a blow job. Most girls before this usually just had it end with sex. I guess I'll always be up for whatever, and it was awesome.

Everyone, that's one piece of advice I can give you. Change it up every now and then, and keep it going. Doing the same thing over and over again loses its interest, and that's where the excitement or desire to want it is. That makes a long-lasting happy couple.

Thick finished me off, and I blew my load. After it was all said and done, Thick laid next to me and asked if I enjoyed it. Now I couldn't think of a better morning, having just added sex to my list, and it was just then going on noon that day. Yeah, I would say that I enjoyed it very much. Thick got up and put her clothes back on. Just before she left the room again, she handed my clothes and smiled good-bye. I got up off the mattress, put my clothes back on, and headed to the door.

Word was waiting at the door and asked what took so long. I told him I got a massage and then had some sex. He looked at me with a discouraged look on his face and told me that it would have been nice if I let him know that I planned to have sex. Then what came out of his mouth next kind of bothered me. He told me that he would have had sex with his girl, too, if he had known.

Now it gets down to another one of my morals. I know that many people out there aren't faithful to the person. My question to you is, "Why the fuck did you get in a relationship then, or why the fuck are you lying to someone about what you did?" We're all human beings, and we all have emotions that we hate having fucked with. I would say the best thing you can do is be honest with the person up-front. If you can be faithful to him or her, it's not worth hurting another person for. That's why I did all of this before I got in a relationship. Now when Word said this, I just kind of shrugged it off because I can't really control what someone else does, but the way I see it, he made the smart decision by not sleeping with her.

We left the massage place, and I told Word that we needed to start heading back because I had to meet up with Spark and Dick. We walked all the way to the check-in place, and I met with my supervisors again. I swear I feel like these people didn't do much else this whole trip except get drunk and check people in and out. I asked if they had seen Spark and Dick check out yet, and they said they were by there just fifteen minutes ago. I thought to myself, "Fuck, I just missed them, and now I have to go look for them."

Looking for people in Thailand isn't the easiest task in the world. Considering the fact that you can do anything and it only cost about two dollars to get a cab and go anywhere, this made things quite difficult for me. I figured I could find them at one of the bars close by, and that was where I started my search. After all, it was time for me to start drinking anyway.

Word and I walked around most of the bar but only stopped to take a glance at them before I settled to stop and have myself a drink. The bar I stopped at caught my attention for a reason. A few tourists were playing this thing that I like to call the Stump Game out front. I'll let you know how some of the bars work in Thailand. The bar keeps all of these random games around the bar, one being Connect Four, another being the Jackpot Game, and the last game being the Stump Game. It's very simple. If you beat the bartender at any of these games, he or she owes you a drink. If you lose, you have to buy the bartender a drink. So if you feeling likely, why not try your luck?

Now Connect Four is easy to explain. If you connect four, you win. If not, you lose. The Jackpot Game consists of rolling dice and trying to be the first one to spell out the word "jackpot" without rolling the same number twice. The Stump Game it where it's at. The Stump Game is played by having everyone stand around a stump with a chipping hammer. Everyone goes around the stump, trying to be the first to get his nail into the stump with his or her chipping hammer. The trick is that you only get one hit per turn. Yeah, it's a great game to play while you're drunk.

I watched everyone playing the game take his turns, and the bartender beat all. Considering it was the middle of the day, I didn't think any of them were drunk enough to not hit the nail, so it just meant the bartender was just that damn good. After watching everyone lose, I thought to myself, "This is something we should bring to America. It would really help bring some of the money a bar might lose in a night back in." I knew I had to try this game at least once.

The crowd around the stump scattered, leaving only the bartender left, collecting her money that she won for her drinks. I walked right up to the bartender and asked if I could challenge her to a game, and she happily accepted my challenge. She pulled two nails out of a box and tapped the nails into the stump, just enough to keep it standing. She handed me my hammer, and we got the game started.

I took my first swing and missed. Go figure I would miss on the first swing. Having to use a chipping hammer all day at work, you think I would be better at it. The bartender took her first swing and hit the nail in halfway. This wasn't looking good for me at all. I took my next swing and got a hit, but I only hit my nail less than a quarter in. The bartender took her next swing and missed. I sure thought luck was on my side now. I took my next swing, and I got another hit, but my nail was only now a quarter of the way in. If I wanted to win this game, I was going to have to get in my nail and fast. The bartender took her next hit and hit her nail almost completely in. I knew I only had a few hits left before she won, so I gave this swing everything I had a missed. Just then, the bartender took her swing and hit her nail all the way in. I was defeated and already had to buy someone else a beer before I got my first one.

I gave the bartender her money for her drink, and we both made our way to our sides of the bar. I took my seat on a barstool next to Word and told him I just got my ass kicked in a game that seemed like it didn't require much thinking at all. Word couldn't help but laugh and told me to try my luck at Connect Four. I thought to myself, "I already got my ass kicked once. Why would I want to embarrass myself further?" I got my beer and enjoyed myself for a second before I told Word that we had to continue looking for Spark and Dick.

I told the bartender thanks for the beer and kicking my ass, and I took my beer right out of the bar with me. One good thing about being in foreign countries is that, in most of them, you can carry open alcohol with you, and there's not much anyone is going to say or do to you.

As soon as I stepped out of the bar, I looked to my right and saw a young Thai woman with light skin, light brown hair, and an innocent look to her. She really stuck out from all of the other Thai woman I had seen so far. She was sweeping the floor to another empty bar, all while drinking a bottle of something. I wanted to know what she had in the bottle so I approached and asked what she was drinking. She told me that it was Thai whiskey and asked if I ever had any. I told her no, and she dropped her broom and ran off.

I assumed that I scared her away because of how quickly she took off. I thought it was an insult that I never drank Thai whiskey before, and I was wondering what I got myself into. I figured that, if I did insult her, I would make up for it by sweeping the rest of the bar out for her. I grabbed the broom and started sweeping the floor. Not even a few seconds later, I overheard a laugh coming from behind me. The woman had returned with two shot glasses in her hand. She asked why I was sweeping the floor. I didn't want to tell her that I thought I just insulted her, so I told her I was trying to make her job easier for her.

The woman then set down the glasses on the table next to the bottle and started to fill the glasses. She told me to stop sweeping the floor and come over to have a drink with her. I have to be honest. Thai people are probably some of the nicest people in the world. It's like they don't have a care in the world and they view everyone as a friend to them. It's a lot different from how we live here at home. I walked over to the table as she took the broom from me and set it down. She then grabbed a drink, handed to me, and told me to drink it. I downed the shot, and I'd be lying if I didn't tell you that Thai whiskey doesn't have a bite to it. I mean, this stuff felt like I had just gotten kicked in the face by a mule.

I set down the glass with a look of my face wondering what she had just given me. She proceeded to laugh and asked if I liked the Thai whiskey. I've tried all kinds of exotic food and alcohols, but nothing that had a bite quite like that to it. I told her that it would take some getting used to if I planned to drink it all the time. For being such a small girl, I was surprised that she could knock it back like she did, but hey, I guess it comes with the culture. I told her thanks for the drink and made my way to find Spark and Dick yet again.

As Word and I started walking back down the street full of bars, he asked me where else I might be able to find Spark and Dick. Honestly at this point, I had no idea where they could have been in this city, and I started to think that I wasn't going to find them. Just as soon as I thought that it would take forever, right at the very end of the street, I saw the two of them walking our way. I still wonder what the chances of that were, but I guess it was bound to happen sooner or later.

Word and I ran down the street to meet up with them and ask how long they had been walking around the city and what time they got here. They told me that it took forever for them to leave and get back into the city because there was some damage done to the path that would have gotten them here and they had to take an alternate route. Then they told me that, because of it, they were having a recall tomorrow at four instead of midnight like it was supposed to be. That meant I had less than twenty-four hours to do everything else I wanted to. It's not like it was much. Besides, I'd just enjoyed the party since. I wasn't ready to leave Thailand. Not yet.

I asked Spark and Dick what their plans were for the rest of the day, and they said they had to do some shopping for souvenirs they needed for themselves and people back home. I told the two of them to meet Word and I back at the check-in station in two hours. We went our separate ways, and now I just had to figure out how to waste two hours of my day. I didn't really have any plans or anything certain I really wanted to do besides just enjoy the bars and party later, so this was going to be interesting seeing what I would get myself into.

As I said, I was walking down the street, and I noticed a random cat that was just walking along the street. Now I was sure this cat didn't have any of its shots, and I probably shouldn't have picked it up, but I did anyway. After I picked up the cat, I made it less than a block down the street, and the next thing I heard was an old Thai lady yelling at me. I had no idea what she wanted from me, but I could tell she sure was angry. She started hitting me with a piece of rolled-up newspaper, still yelling at me. She wasn't speaking English so I had no idea what I wanted. I thought I probably just looked like somebody she knew. Everyone around was looking at me and watching this old lady hit me with a rolled-up newspaper. Then it clicked in my head that it was her cat.

I put the cat on the ground, and the lady still kept yelling at me. I tried to calmly explain to the lady that she could have her cat back and I thought it was a stray. She then picked up her cat off the ground and hit with me the newspaper a few more times before she walked away. Lesson learned from this. Don't pick up random cats in Thailand. Word started laughing at me and asked how I got myself into these situations. I told him it all comes with the skill and experience over time and said that he'd get good at it, too, one day.

Word and I stated on our journey again, walking around town until I came up to another unusual sight I had never seen before. In fact, I had never heard of this before I went to Thailand. I saw these tourists putting their feet into a tank of water that was full of these tiny fish, and the fish were eating at their feet. I told Word that, if he were willing to try it, so was I. He agreed, and I asked the man running the place how much it cost. Of course, it was cheap again. It only cost me a dollar for both the fish and foot massage. You can't find a better deal than that anywhere in America. Word and I both paid the man, took off our shoes, and dunked our feet right into the water.

The feeling of the fish is very different because it doesn't feel like they're biting, but yet you can feel them again on your feet. The whole point is to have the fish eat the dead skin off your foot to help smooth off any callous or corns that you might have. I can't believe that this is illegal in America. I'm sure that someone could make a killing off people if they brought it Stateside. Our feet stayed in the tank for the next several minutes or so before the man came by and told me us to take out our feet and move to the massage chairs.

I already had one massage earlier that day that came with a little something extra, and I knew by the setup that this massage wouldn't offer the same thing, but I was okay with that. The only thought I had was that I was going to be so relaxed that night that I might not even make it out to the bars. Word and I took our seats in the massage chairs, and two beautiful Thai women came out of the back and gave us our foot massage. By the time the massage was done, I didn't want to get up, and I most likely wouldn't have if I had to meet Spark and Dick in a little bit. The massage was over, and like I said before, nothing extra came with this massage. I tipped the massage therapist, put my shoes back on, and made my way out of the store.

The only thing that was left to do now was waste the rest of the time that I had until I had to meet up again with Spark and Dick. I really had no idea what to do at this point to waste time so Word and I spent the rest of the time looking at all of the random trinkets that Thailand had to offer. Thailand is probably number one on my list of places I would recommend for anyone if he or she planned to do any trinket shopping. After all the time was wasted, we were told it was time to head back to the check-in spot.

Word and I arrived back at the check-in spot, and to my surprise, different people were working. I asked the two new people where the last two supervisors were. I didn't believe their answer because they told me that they were sleeping. "Yeah, I often like to get drunk in my sleep, too," was the thought I had passing through my head. Not long after Word and I arrived, Spark and Dick showed up. I could finally get started on the drunken day I had ahead of me that I already planned out.

Originally, it was just going to be Spark, Dick, and I heading out, but I felt that we couldn't leave Word behind by himself so we took him with us. We all signed out together and left to go and find ourselves a cab. Now remember how I said on the first night that the cabdriver drove us to a hotel in the next town over. I remembered why just then. It was because that was the same hotel we already made reservations at for the night we planned to stay out. See my great idea was that we would stay in the next town over where no one we knew would be so we could party all night and not have to worry someone telling us we couldn't. Little did I know later, the same reason would become a lot more important.

The four of us walked out to the main road and hailed the first tuk-tuk we saw. I was so relieved to know that it wasn't the same two people who drove us around the first day. We all got into the back of the tuk-tuk and started making our way over to Rayong, the next city over from Jomtien. If I would have known that Rayong was as dead as it was, I would have never suggested that we stay there. Rayong only really has one main street to it, and all of the businesses close very early at night, and there isn't really much of a nightlife in Rayong.

We arrived at the hotel and didn't make the cabdriver wait around for us because we assumed that everything we needed would be right there. The hotel itself looked amazing. Honestly, it could have been a resort that deserved its own island. Even at the check-in desk, they greeted us with a glass of champagne. It was how I imagined movie stars get treated whenever they walked into places. The day was turning out to be really good. The front desk checked us into our rooms and handed us our room keys. We even had a guy offering to carry our stuff and show us to our room. I can't believe I got all of this for only fifty dollars.

We got to our room and set down all of our stuff. I even took the box of Viagra I still had in my pocket and set it down on one of the counters in the room. The room itself wasn't as big as what I thought it would be. It had two full-sized beds in it and a couch that someone could sleep on. The one thing about hotel room that gets me every time is the fact how there is a window between the shower and the main room that you can open up. I guess it's a good idea if you want to watch the TV while you are taking a shower, but other than that, I'm sure no one else wants to watch you take a shower. The view outside of the room wasn't bad. You could see the mountains and feel the nice breeze as it came right off the ocean from the beach. I'm sure I was meant to live there.

Spark and Dick still needed to get ready for the night, and I didn't feel like sitting around, so I told them I was going to make a beer run. As I mentioned before, there is only one main street in Rayong. It starts at the end of the hotel and connects to the road that takes you right through the city. This main street in Rayong consists of a few restaurants and massage places with the one and only liquor store being at the very end of the street. Of course, I would have to walk past all these people, trying to drag me into their stores to get where I wanted to go. It's a lot like having that family member who always wants to borrow money from you. You don't want to say no because you like them, but you don't want to say yes because you are tired of their crap.

I got all the way to the liquor store without giving into any of the demands from all of the vendors of the stores before this one. The only things I bought from this liquor store were a six-pack of beer and a bottle of Thai whiskey. I figured tonight would be a good night to try to get used to it. Besides if I couldn't drink it, I was sure that either Spark or Dick would.

After paying for the alcohol, I made my way back to the hotel room, once again dodging vendors left and right. Once inside the hotel room, I put all of the stuff I just bought in the fridge, and I was ready to head out.

The only problem was that Dick was taking his time, like he normally did, and this was getting to be annoying. Something about him gave me a bad feeling about that night, but I was too into party mode that I didn't care.

Dick was finally done getting ready for the night, and we made our way out of the hotel room. As we reached the main floor, we say two women come running down the steps. These women were both white with blonde hair and blue eyes. At first, I would have mistaken them for any part of the world until I asked what they were running from. One woman happened to be a little bit older, and she replied in her Australian accent. And I knew right where they were from then. She said they were trying to get away from the younger girl's mom because they wanted to go out and party. The younger girl couldn't have been much older than twenty years of age. The whole night, we ended up calling the old one "Mom" and the younger one "Blondie."

We asked the two of them where they were heading, and they both replied at the same time, saying they were heading to the bar district in Partong. The whole goal for the night was to party away from Jomtien, but by the way that Rayong looked, I knew this wasn't going to happen. Spark, Dick, Word, and I all talked it out and said, "Screw it! We'll head back with the two

Aussies to Jomtien and hang out with them." They seemed like fun people anyway. We asked the two Aussies if they wouldn't mind our company for the night, and they were more than happy to have us come along with them.

Now the one kind of girl I never slept with that I've always wanted to is an Australian girl. I'm not sure what it is about Australian woman, but I find them to be the most beautiful women on the whole planet. I kind of figured that I would get the chance to do it tonight, so going with the two of them didn't seem like such a bad option.

Mom led us to the main road and flagged down a tuk-tuk for us. The tuk-tuk pulled over to the side of the road, and we all got in. I thought we would have been dropped off right in the middle of the whole bar district, but Mom and us got dropped off on the outskirts of town, and we had to walk all the way to the bar district.

The first bar we ended up at wasn't even done being built yet. I mean, it was supposed to be a big bar. You could see all the way in the back, but they only had the front bar open. This was where Dick started his drinking hard right away. I lost count of how much he had to drink at this bar because I focused on trying to get with Blondie. Spark and Word ran across the street to a store so they could finally get Word's SIM card. I kind of felt bad for the guy. I hung out with him all day, and he just now got his SIM card. It was already dark outside. I guess it was the least we could have done for him. After all, he wasn't going to be staying with us all night.

Dick pretty much tried to challenge the bartender to every game the bar had to offer and kept losing so he had to keep buying drinks. For every drink he bought the bartender, he bought himself one as well. Spark and Word finally came back from the store, and my focus was still set on trying to get with Blondie. That was until Mom stepped in and asked me what my plans were with Blondie. Well, I was honest with her, and I said I'd never been with an Australian woman before. Mom just laughed and said we'd see how the night went.

Just then, I heard the sounds of arguments in the background. Dick had lost a game against the bartender, and she told him that he owed her a drink. Dick believed that she cheated and didn't think it was fair that he had to pay her. Long story short, we didn't stay at that bar much longer. All of us left the bar and started our journey to the bar district again. I felt it was time to get back at Dick for everything he did in the past and just now getting us kicked out of the bar.

Dick was walking ahead of the group, and I hung back behind everyone with Spark. I proceeded to run up to everyone on the street and point out Dick to all. I told everyone for about a mile that Dick loved lady boys and asked, if they knew of any, to send them his way. It was something that I probably shouldn't have done, but with all of the things he'd done to me and everyone else, he kind of deserved it.

By the time we reached the bar distract in Jomtien, Dick had about five lady boys following him, and he couldn't figure out why. That was score one for Flynt that night. This wouldn't be the only time that we tried to set up Dick with a lady boy. We actually tried one or two more times until he caught on that we were trying to get him with one. We stopped at a random bar in the middle of Jomtien, and Mom bought us all our first round. I guess buying a round over in Thai is about the same as buying yourself one drink over here in America. So it's not like much money was spent, but it was still a nice gesture.

We all got our drinks, and sure enough, Dick kept acting like a dick the whole time. Spark and I started to think to ourselves, "If I have to put up with this shit all night, it's not going to last long." I mean, it wasn't like I was much better the other night; however, everyone else was drunk with me except for one person. I was standing outside of the bar with my back turned to the crowd, and not long after, someone tapped me on my shoulder. I turned around and saw Psycho. Psycho had actually cashed in his vacation days so he wouldn't have to do any work while we were in Thailand. They weren't going to let him do it, but they had no choice. He had already bought his wife a plane ticket to Thailand, and they knew the ticket was refundable so he found a way to beat the system.

This was actually the first time I had ever met Psycho's wife, who was nothing like him. She was a calm lady with a slender body and long brown hair, and she was about as tall as Psycho was. She was a medical student in college working on her master's. What can I say? Psycho was pretty much set for life. I know. Right out of all places to meet someone's wife, it's in a country where you can do anything. Psycho and I never mentioned anything about what had just happened in the Philippines. We figured at this point that it was just water under the bridge. Psycho had also been to Thailand before, and some of his stories were crazy so it was kind of funny to see how calm he was in front of his wife.

Psycho asked me what I was doing for the night, and I told him I got a hotel room with Spark and Dick and we planned to stay out all night partying. Psycho told us about a bar at the end of the street called Rock Party that had a live band playing that he was going to check out.

I ran the idea past everyone, and all said they wanted to go check it out. That was everyone except for Dick. He had a bet going on with Spark that he could get this random tourist girl to go back to the hotel with him, and Spark called bullshit on it. After all, the girl was by herself without any of her friends around. She was about as drunk as Dick was, and if anyone saw her leave with us, trust me, Dick would have been all over the news the next day. Dick was so convinced that he could that he took the girl to the next bar with us.

I asked Psycho how he was enjoying his time in Thailand. He said that, so far, he and his wife spent it at the beach and hiking in the jungle. It sounded like a romantic getaway to me. That was until he got to the part about the snake show. Now if you recall the pussy show I talked about earlier, it's kind of along the same lines, but instead of vaginas being involved in everything, it was snakes. By snakes, I mean actual live snakes and not penises. Psycho said it was the same thing for him. He went to the show, and no one else was volunteering, so he was just drunk enough to do it himself. He said they brought him up onstage, and he'd never forget what happened next.

He said that the man who was hosting the show had him stand center stage, asking him where he was from and why he was in Thailand. The man then asked Psycho if he were ready for what happened next.

Psycho, of course, responded by saying, "Bring it on!"

The man then came out with a tub, and the contents of what was in it were unknown. The man opened the case and told Psycho to relax. The man then proceeded to pull out snakes by the handful and wrapped Psycho in the snakes. Psycho was sure that some, if not most, of these snakes were poisonous, but hey, that's the way things go in Thailand.

Psycho had all of the snakes wrapped on him, and the man asked how he was feeling. Psycho didn't respond to the man because he knew he didn't want to get bitten. Just then, the man decided he would make things more interesting and started hitting the snakes on their heads, as if it were going to make things better. I swear the man was trying to kill Psycho. After the man got done hitting the snakes and pissing them off, he then encouraged Psycho to hit the snakes. Psycho just yelled at the man and told him he was fucking crazy and to get the snakes off him.

By the time Psycho was done telling me this story, we had reached the next bar, and I was afraid I wouldn't be able to hold down my drink because of the laughing I had going on at the time. The whole time we were walking down the street, Dick was still giving the moves to the girl he met at the bar, and Spark just kept telling Dick that it wasn't going to happen. Word hadn't really said much all night until we got rid of him. I'm not sure what was wrong with the guy. I hope he enjoyed himself.

The bar Rock Party looked just like it sounded. It was designed to look like you just stepped into hell and it was a never-ending rock concert. The waitresses dressed up in nurse outfits and walked around with plastic syringes full of booze. I'm not quite sure what was in the syringes, but whatever it was, it tasted good. I figured I would pay back Mom for buying me and everyone else a drink, so I bought a round for her and Blondie at the same time Psycho bought me my first round so it was like I never spent any money at all.

I was still trying to get with Blondie, and Psycho asked me the story about the two Aussies. I told them we met them outside of the hotel we were staying at so we decided to party with them. I am sure that everyone has partied with random people every now and then. Dick was still spending his time trying to get with the same girl, but now it looked like he was failing bad, and all I could see was Spark laughing at Dick for failing. Word didn't say a word and kept to himself the whole time we were in the bar. Psycho and I, on the other hand, were going all out.

This bar had a great deal going on, buy one drink and get one free all night. I can't think of any bars in America that run a special like that ever, but they should. I bet they would sell a lot. Psycho and I decided it was time to drink a piña colada. Before Muscles got fired, it was our dream to hang out on the beach all day and drink piña coladas out of a coconut. That was actually our dream when we were in Mexico, but we ended up sleeping with prostitutes instead. Muscles had actually left us earlier in the year because he got into an argument with one of or supervisors. The supervisor called him a dumbass and told Muscles that he didn't know anything about his job. This pissed off Muscles a great deal, and Muscles threatened to put him in a coma. I'm not going to lie. If you get butt hurt over someone telling you that he is going to put you in a coma, I think it's time you man the fuck up. So Muscles, if you're reading this, that piña colada was for you, and I hope that, where you are, you are living out your dreams.

Psycho and I both downed our piña coladas, and then we ordered our next round of beers. Just as soon as we got our beers in our hands, the words "Power Hour" showed up on the screen. Now, our power hour was completely different from the bar's power hour. The bar's power hour consisted of all drinks being half off, including the buy-one-get-one-free deal. Psycho and I did our version of the power hour, and by the time we got our shirts off, we were told to put them back on or leave the bar. So it was a language barrier that messed us up. Oh, well. I'm sure more people would have joined in after a while.

Not long after the attempt of the shirtless power hour, Spark approached me and told me it was time to go. I sat there thinking there was no way we could just leave. I was having the time of my life. He told me that Dick pretty much failed at trying to get the girl he was talking to, and Spark didn't want to be around the Aussies much longer. He wanted to break off and do his own thing. I told Spark that I was good for whatever, so Spark went and told Dick we were leaving. I told Word that we were going to drop him off at the check-in spot.

Trying to get Dick to leave the bar and girl behind he was talking to was no easy task. He kept telling Spark that he was in and going to be taking the girl home tonight. So we lied to Dick, the Aussies, and Psycho and told them all that we would be back. We told the Aussies that we had to go back to the hotel to get something we forgot. In truth, we wanted to get away from them. Mom walked us outside, hailed down a tuk-tuk for us, and told us to get in. To make it look like we weren't lying, we hopped into the tuk-tuk, but once we were out of sight, we made the guy turn around and drop us off at the check-in spot.

We got to the check-in spot, and two different people were working. I was surprised that they were actually rotating through people who were most likely drunk at this point. I figured I should ask where our supervisors were so we knew to avoid them. Yeah, that didn't happen. They told us that they were out in the bar district somewhere having a few drinks. I love how they could go to work drunk, but if I did it, they would have lit my world up. We signed Word back in and told him to enjoy the rest of the night. I felt bad just leaving the guy like that, but plans were already set and in motion. Spark, Dick, and I all signed out and left again to go back to the bars.

Sure enough, as soon as we turned the corner, there were our supervisors, standing right there. It was the same bar they were at before, but this time, they were outside of the bar playing the Stump Game. They both had random girls hanging all over them again, and they were drunk yet again, knowing they would have to work again soon. I really wish I would have gotten pictures. Dick, being drunk like he was, ran right up to the Stump Game and wanted to join in. This started to piss off Spark and me because the last thing we wanted to do was hang out with our supervisors. So I figured I would have some fun with this situation if I could.

I went right up to the girl who was playing the game, standing right next to Dick. I told the girl that, if she hit Dick in the face with the hammer, I would give her thirty dollars American or a hundred dollars in Thai. The lady never went for it, so if I figured I could get her to go for it, I would at least get to someone.

I looked right at my supervisor and said, "Well, that's a nice ring you got on there. How's the wife and kids doing?"

I'm really serious. Cheating is one way to piss me off quick. My supervisor looked at me and told me to mind my own business and to get the hell away from him. Spark and I pulled Dick away from the table and went on our way.

Dick went running down the street until he got stopped by a guy handing out business cards, or at least I thought that was what they were. They were actually discount coupons for free drinks at several of the bars in the area. We took as many as we could and went on our way. We let Dick lead us to all the bars, but at every bar, it was the same thing. You get a drink and down it, and then it's on to the next bar. We must have hit three or four different bars doing this. I swear that it's the greatest place on earth. You can't beat free drinks, let alone free anything.

Back on the street again, we started looking for the busiest bar in the whole area. A random white guy on the street stopped us. He was walking around now with a shirt on and a pair of sunglasses. I wouldn't doubt that this guy was rolling on something. He was out in the middle of the street advertising his bar he called the White Room. Now I'm not going to lie. It sounded really racist, and it sounded like a room in an insane asylum. We asked the man if he knew of any other busy bars in the area, and of course, he tried to push us to go to the White Room. Once the kid saw that we weren't budging, he told us about the bar right next door called Club Famous. I'll never forget that name.

Club Famous at the time was Jomtien's number-one nightclub in the whole city. Knowing how the bar and nightclub world work, I'm pretty sure that something else has taken over as number one. Club Famous was right in the middle of the bar district, and its opening sat back a little bit from the rest of the bars. You had to walk up a flight of stairs to get inside, but once you were in, you could hardly move or hear yourself think. Once the three of us got to the top of the stairs, several bouncers stopped us for a quick pat-down just to make sure we weren't bringing any weapons in the club with us.

After the quick pat-down, we were led right to the bar to get our drinks. You couldn't get into the rest of the club unless you had a drink. I'm not going to lie. This is another smart idea most bars or clubs should incorporate into their businesses. I'm not going to lie. We probably should have cut Dick off, but it was Thailand, so why not let him go all out?

The three of us got our drinks and headed on into the club. This place was packed, and yet somehow we were the only white people in the whole club. I didn't know this at the time, but this club was actually full of prostitutes. I thought it was just a random hangout spots for the locals, but no, it turned out that this was where most of the street prostitutes hung out in their normal clothes.

We somehow managed to make it all the way across the club even with the poor lighting and almost having no room to move. Dick leaned over to both Spark and I and told us that he was going to get a girl here to go back to the hotel with him. Now, I've watched people crash and burn in bars while trying to pick up women, but Dick tonight made it look like he wrote the book on how to fail at picking up women.

He was so drunk that he would just started randomly dancing with any woman he was close to until they told him to get away from him. Once they wanted nothing to do with him, he would yell at them and say they were missing out. So before a fight broke out, I would run up to the girl he just got done yelling at and say that Dick liked lady boys and not to mind him at all. Yeah, I got him again that night.

I was standing in the middle of the club, trying to calm down one of the girls that Dick just pissed off, and I turned around to see her. This girl was more beautiful than any other Thai girl I had seen on my whole trip. She had a nice tan body, dark hair with highlights, and a lip piercing that gave her a rock-and-roll image. As soon as I saw her, my goal was set, and I knew I was taking her to the hotel with me. I walked right up to her and asked what her name was. It was so hard to hear in the bar, so I had to have her repeat it a few times to me. She spoke in broken English, but I didn't care. She was hot. She said her name was Tia and she was there with all of her friends. I did manage to get a few pictures and even a video of the bar that night of the party that was going on.

I set Dick up with one of her friends and told him not to fuck it up this time. Spark didn't go for anyone because he was married, and I respect the decision he made on that. After about an hour or so of drinking and partying, it was time to get heading on back to the hotel. I knew that Spark was tired because he had been up all night before working and didn't get any sleep. I asked Tia if she were going to come back to my hotel with me and everyone else.

Tia asked me how much money I had, and I pulled out another thirty dollars. She gladly accepted it and packed up her things to leave. I told Dick to pay his girl so we could get out of the club and be on our way.

I turned back to Spark and told him I was ready whenever he was. Spark slammed the rest of his beer, and off we went with Spark, Dick, Tia, her friend, and I going back to the hotel. At this point, I could really care less who saw me with who. After all, I already told everyone I worked with that I slept with prostitutes, and I wasn't trying to keep it a secret. In fact, most people encouraged it because they felt they could never do it themselves.

Once again back into another tuk-tuk, on our way back to the hotel, Dick was so drunk that he couldn't stop arguing with Spark over the fact that Dick still thought he could have had the girl from earlier. That would explain the reason why Dick ended up with a prostitute.

I had only been in Thailand for three days, and I already was going to be with three different prostitutes. I don't know if you would consider that a problem or a good time. All I know is that, if I lived in Thailand, I would probably be broke after going home with a different girl every night. I guess it's a good thing that I don't live in Thailand after all.

As soon as the tuk-tuk pulled up to the hotel, security escorted us all to the front desk. I couldn't believe that, if you get caught bringing a prostitute back to your hotel room at this particular hotel, they made you pay for her to be here. I'm not going to lie. It's a load of shit. If I've already paid for the hotel room, it's my own damn business what I do in my hotel room. Why do I have to pay to bring my prostitute in the room with me?

I argued with the front desk for quite some time about this, but they weren't budging. I guess it's written down somewhere in a handbook and they have to live up to their company policy. I paid the fee and went on my way. I wasn't too happy about having to pay the extra fee, and I was going to let them know it. We got to the room, and Spark told me he was going to take a walk and have a smoke or two while everything was going on. I told him good luck and not to get lost. Once we got into the room, Dick took her girl right out to the balcony because he himself wanted to have a smoke as well. I didn't waste any time. I went right to my bed and started getting her clothes off.

Once I had all of Tia's clothes off, the sex started right away. I didn't last long until we got our first noise complaint. Apparently while I was have sex with Tia, the bedpost was slamming too hard again the wall, and it woke up the people in the room next to us. The first complaint was in the form of a phone call, but the man on the other end was speaking in Thai. I couldn't understand him, so I just agreed and hung up the phone. After I hung up the phone, Dick came walking back in with his girl and took her right to the bathroom. Before he closed the door to the bathroom, I heard the sound of something rustling in the background. I didn't think anything of it so I went back to having sex with Tia.

Again during sex, the sound of someone knocking on the door interrupted me. I figured it wasn't anybody important, so I ignored it. The person knocked again, so I tried to ignore it once again. There was a third knock on the door, and I thought that Spark might have just misplaced his room key and was trying to get in. So I got up out of the bed and answered the door. It turned out that it was another one of the security guards, and I got my second noise complaint of the night for the same reason. I thought to myself, "There is no way I'm going to be able to have sex with Tia tonight if this shit keeps happening." So I did the only thing I could think of. I pulled the bed away from the wall.

After I had the bed all situated, I went back to having sex with Tia, and of course, it wasn't long before I got my third noise complaint. I already moved the bed away from the wall, and I highly doubt the people in the room next to me had hearing equivalent to that of a dog. The phone rang, and I answered it. This time, Tia grabbed the phone out of my hand and spoke to the man in Thai. What she said to them, I have no idea, but I do know that they never called or knocked on our door again. I went back to having sex with Tia, and this time, I tried to make it as quiet as possible. If you never tried to have sex quietly, I'll let you know right now that it completely sucks. You are limited to what you can and can't do, and it's not enjoyable in any way. So yeah, I pretty much took a prostitute home that I really wanted to have sex with, and I couldn't even enjoy it.

The sex finally ended, and I was able to cum after all, even though it sucked because of the noise complaints, but I made it work. Not long after I got done, Spark came walking back into the room and fell onto his bad, and he was asleep in a matter of seconds. Dick came out of the bathroom, walked over to my bed, and tried to steal the blanket right off my bed. I told him to let go of it before I kicked his ass. He let go of the blanket and told me he was cold. I told him to put his clothes back on if he were cold. Dick walked over to the couch and passed out completely naked.

Now that everyone was asleep, I felt bad that Tia's friend was standing there by herself so I asked Tia if she wanted her friend to join in. Tia took this the wrong way and thought I wanted to just have sex with her friends, so she climbed out of my bed and told her friend to get in. I figured either way that I'd go for another round of sex, but I didn't know how long it was going to take. I started getting Tia's friend's clothes off, and shortly after, Tia came walking back up with the box of Viagra that I took out of my pocket earlier. I noticed that the pills were out of the box and another one was missing. It turned out that the rustling noise in the background from earlier was actually Dick taking one of the Viagras out of the package. Once again, Dick was doing things he shouldn't have been doing.

I told Tia and her friend that Dick's dick didn't work so well and he needed to take those in order to have sex. I probably should not have said that, but just as I said before, it was another one of those things he had coming to him. I mean, look at the guy now. He just got done with a prostitute, and he was passed out on couch with no clothes on and a rock-hard dick. It sounded like the rock-and-roll lifestyle to me. Tia put down the box and then jumped in bed with Spark. Now I'm not really sure if anything happened between the two of them. I wasn't paying attention, but I'm sure that nothing happened because Spark valued his relationship too much to blow it all away like that.

Tia's friend and I had sex, and once again, I had to keep everything quiet to keep from pissing off the people next door and getting kicked out of the hotel. So this marked number four of all the prostitutes I had sex with in Thailand. I got to sleep with four different prostitutes for only the price of three. Not only did Thailand have drink specials, but they had specials on girls, too. There was no way that it could get better than this. At least that was what I thought at the time being.

I got done having sex with Tia's friend, and I drifted off into sleep, knowing that my last whole day in Thailand was spent the way I wanted it to be. That was until Dick screwed me over once again.

Both Tia and her friend woke me up. They had turned on all the lights, and they were pissed. Tia's friend pointed at me and said I owed her money. I kept thinking to myself that I didn't owe her shit. Dick was the one who took her from the bar. He paid her.

She pointed at me again and said, "You owe me money."

I looked right back at her and said, "I don't owe you shit. Fuck off."

Now this was when Tia told me the truth. She pointed at Dick and said he never paid her. "So you owe me money."

Once again, Dick struck again, and I had to bail his ass out of another situation. I jumped out of bed and put my clothes back on. I walked over to Dick, still passed out on the couch, and wanted to tear his head off. If there were one person that night who needed to get his ass kicked, it was him. I checked my wallet, and it was empty. Spark fell asleep with his wallet in his pocket, and I wasn't about ready to wake him up.

I looked around for Dick's clothes, and I finally found his pants. I took the wallet out of his pocket, and I knew this was going to happen. Dick had no money in his wallet so he never planned to pay his prostitute. Dick had fucked me once again in a matter of seconds.

Now, I have never had my ass kicked by a pimp, although I know it would make for a funny story that I still plan on having it happen. I was sure it was going to happen on this night, but it never did. Instead, I took the alternate route. I had to take Tia and her friend with me to an ATM so I could pay them to leave. I grabbed my room key, and down to the main road we went. Trying to get a tuk-tuk on a pass-through road at four in the morning is no easy task. I swear I spent a half hour alone trying to get a tuk-tuk to stop and pick us up.

Finally after it seemed like there wouldn't be a tuk-tuk coming for miles, I started walking. I felt that this was going to be a trip that I wasn't going to come back from. If it weren't, at least I could say I enjoyed my last few days on earth, and my predictions of Dick getting me killed in some way was becoming true.

Just as I started walking, a tuk-tuk pulled over to the side of the road, and the three of us got it. This whole trip to the ATM, I was pissed off at the fact that I got woken up earlier to find out that Dick had screwed me over yet again. Tia and her friend were laughing the whole ride to the ATM as if the whole thing were a big joke to them.

The ride to the ATM started getting shady because the driver had driven past at least twenty ATMs already. I knew to myself by now that tonight was going to be the night that I disappeared or died. Next thing I knew, the tuk-tuk driver stopped right outside of a 7-Eleven, the only sign of civilization around in a place where no one seemed to inhabit anymore. I got out of the tuk-tuk, and both Tia and her friend waited for me. I used the ATM and pulled out another thirty dollars. I was so glad that I got to pay for someone else to have sex.

After I got the money, I got back into the tuk-tuk, but I refused to give them the money until I got dropped back off at the hotel. The last thing I wanted them to do was take my money and leave me stranded in the middle of nowhere.

The cab ride back was even worse because I thought to myself how I was going to get back at Dick for this shit. Tia and her friend did the same thing on the ride back and acted like it was a big joke to them. I couldn't wait to get out of that tuk-tuk and get back to the hotel room. The tuk-tuk had pulled up to the hotel, and I couldn't have gotten out and away from Tia fast enough. Just as soon as I was about to walk back into the hotel, Tia looked at me and said goodnight.

I thought, "She has got to be shitting me. The two of them just woke me up to make me pay them to leave, and one of the guys I was with just screwed me over another time in my life."

I looked at Tia and said, "What the fuck does it matter if I have a good night anymore?"

And I walked away. I probably could have ended that a lot better, but sometimes when you are pissed about things, you don't think so clearly.

I made my way back to the hotel room and went back to sleep for the rest of the night. The next day, I was the first one awake so I took a shower and got all my things together. It was getting close to checkout time at the hotel so I woke up both Spark and Dick. Trust me. When Dick woke up, I let him have it. I told them both how I got woken up in the middle of the night to go to a ATM with two prostitutes so I could pay them to leave because Dick had no money.

I look back at the situation now, and I laugh at it, but at the time, it was the worst thing that could have happened. I asked Dick why he had no money, and he told me that he never planned to pay Tia's friend in the first place. Just so everyone knows. Prostitutes aren't free, and if you think they are, you have another thing coming your way.

Dick put on his clothes and stepped outside on the balcony to have a cigarette. I looked at Spark and told him that I didn't want to know if anything happened between him and Tia, and if they did, don't tell me about them. We never talked about that night again.

We all gathered our things and left the hotel room. We checked out of the hotel and made our way back to Jomtien. Since we had to be back early that day anyway, there wasn't really a lot that we wanted to do. I quickly considered sleeping with just one more prostitute and setting a record at sleeping with five different prostitutes in a matter of three and a half days, but I guess things don't work out the way you want them to.

Spark, Dick, and I all made our way to the check-in spot, and sure enough, our supervisors were working, most likely drunk or hungover, I assumed. We checked back in and got on the bus to take us back. Once I got back, it was right back to work.

That was how my whole time in Thailand was spent, and I enjoyed every second of it, even though I don't remember much of the first day. I mean, where else can you sleep with four different prostitutes, blow up a beach, get blacked-out drunk and left for dead, and only spend $300? One day, I plan to make it back to Thailand and hopefully do some more sightseeing along with the partying, but I can't make any promises. My advice to anyone is that, if you ever get a chance to go to Thailand, take it. You will have the time of your life, but create your own adventure.

So this time around, I learned this about prostitutes. Always have your money up front, and this goes both ways. Prostitutes, get the money up front before services are rendered so you don't have to go with someone to an ATM or create a scene. For those who plan to sleep with a prostitute, have the money up front so this way you don't have to take your prostitute to an ATM with you.

Also, I've learned not to have Dick around on anymore of my adventures because I just wind up getting screwed in the end.

THE ADDRESS

After Thailand, we made a few more stops in other countries, but there was nothing that exciting to talk about. I didn't sleep with anyone overseas after Thailand; however, I did see some fucked-up shit. I saw one place where they had the women chained to the bed, and I felt this was immoral and wanted nothing to do with these people. It goes back to my belief that the only reason why you ever get into prostitution is because you want to get into it. If anyone ever forces you to get into prostitution, fuck that person. He doesn't deserve to have you in his life.

The crazy overseas adventure ended, and all of work was complete. The whole crew made it back to Oregon, including everyone from all our supervisors to even Ops, Old, and Swamp. And yes, even Dick managed to come back alive. I wasn't back for even a few weeks, and I was already wanting to get into something. I'm not going to lie. After being over on the other side of the world and seeing how they live, it makes you really appreciate how good you have it back here at home. I think that everyone should take a trip to a Third World country and see exactly how the other side lives.

I had finally turned twenty-one, the legal drinking age in the United States. This day started off just like any other boring day did back at home. I woke up, went to work, performed my job, and went home at the end of the day. The only difference now was that I had a new roommate living with me, and I started my awesome drinking adventure. My roommate was a skinny guy who stood about five-foot-eight. He had a shaved head and a pair of thick reading glasses. He had a thing for basketball and blasting music extremely loud, but it never bothered me as long as it was off by the time I went to sleep.

Every day when my roommate and I got off work, we would run to the liquor store really quick to pick up a twelve-pack of beer each, go home, and get drunk. It started to feel like life was on repeat for a while. One the weekends, everyone was having a party after the shitty workweek we would have. So even if I weren't hanging out with my roommate for the night, I was at someone's house doing the exact same thing.

The beer was bought, and we proceeded to get as drunk as we could. Now I had been overseas very close to a year, and I never had a chance to check out the Internet in the other countries. Let alone using the websites to find any prostitutes overseas never once crossed my mind. Once the beer started flowing, however, the idea of checking websites started to seem like a better idea with every beer I took down. About over fifth or sixth beer in, my roommate stopped and asked me who I was texting on my phone. I don't know why people get this assumption when I'm drinking, but everyone always assumes that I'm texting someone even if I'm checking my bank account.

Now normally I wouldn't come out in the open with the fact that I sleep with prostitutes, but I figured that, if this guy were going to be my roommate, he should know about the kind of shit that I get into. I mean, there were many people from our work crew who slept with someone overseas, and they might have paid for it in some way, but when we got back Stateside, everyone turned into a model citizen. Not me. I figured I wasn't changing for any reason, and besides, it wasn't like I hadn't slept with a prostitutes in the States before. I knew the rules, and I knew what would happen if I got caught. That was a risk that I was willing to take.

I was completely truthful with my roommate and told him exactly what I was doing, and I was considering sleeping with a prostitute that night. I figured I had to. I hadn't slept with one since I'd been back, and I was getting bored and needed some adventure in my life. I never would have thought this to be my roommate's reaction, but as soon as I told him the truth, he instantly got excited and wanted to sleep with one, too. I'm not one to corrupt people, let alone invite them to engage in illegal activity with me. If I go down, hey, it's my own stupid fault, but if someone else went down because of me, that would be something that would stick with me forever.

I just kind of laughed off the remark my roommate made and carried on with looking to see what the website would have to offer. That was until I came across this girl advertising herself that just grabbed my attention and would not let go. Now sometimes the pictures on the websites can be misleading, and sure, there have been cases where the person on the website turns out to be someone else. Luckily, that has never happened to me, and I plan to keep it that way. The girl in the picture was a knockout. She had long, platinum blonde hair, blue eyes, a perfectly oval-shaped face, and lips that looked like they could do some damage in a good way. I had no idea who this woman was, but I knew I had to fuck her that night.

I guess I was sucked into the picture for too long because my roommate had to throw a bottle cap at me to get my attention. I jumped out of my tractor beam state and told him I found the woman I was going to be with that night. I handed him my phone and showed him the picture. I knew I shouldn't have done this because it only piqued his interest more. Now I was going to have to try and talk him out of it so I could go alone. No matter what I said to him, he didn't budge. He was still interested in going. I even tried to convince him that she could have been a cop, and he still didn't care. I couldn't let him throw away his life and his job if anything bad happened to us, so I did the next best thing I could think of. I was going to have to make him drink himself to sleep.

So before he was done with the beer he already had, I handed him his next one. I kept telling him to drink because, if we were doing this, he was going to have to be good and drunk. I wish we would have had more beer left because it would have been easier to get him to a point of wanting to fall asleep. I was working with only the last six beers he had left, and I was determined to make this work. I couldn't stop looking at the pictures on the website as my only motivation to get my roommate drunk and keep myself awake. I knew I was going to see this woman tonight no matter what the cost.

We had finally reached the last of our beers, and my roommate was starting to look like he was going to fall asleep. My plan was working now. I just needed the first part of it to be over. I really wish I would have thought about the amount of alcohol that I was taking down because it would later could back to help me and kick my ass at the exact same time. I was finishing my last beer and looking at the ad one last time. I swear I glanced away from only a few minutes, and when I looked up again, sure enough, there was my roommate passed out in his chair. I grabbed my phone and walked into the next room so I could make the phone call I needed to.

I dialed the number on that ad, and sure enough, it was all kicking in again—the fast heartbeats, the nervousness, and even the debate in my head if I should hang up or not. This was the break from the ordinary I was looking for. Three rings went by, and the woman from the ad picked up the phone. She sounded just like how I imagined her to. The soft voice that made every word come out of her mouth seemed like it was a Siren singing to me. You know, those mystical creatures that lured in pirates with their singing. Right then, I knew I was committed, even if it were a setup. I didn't care. It would have all been worth it. Siren. Let's call her Siren.

The conversation wasn't much different from all the other. We never asked for each other's name, and she asked where I was coming from. I told her that I lived in the next town over, which was about a fifteen-minute drive from where I was. She told me that her price was $200 and to give me a call when I was on my way so she could give me directions to her apartment.

The only problem was that I was drunk and I sure as shit could not drive myself anywhere. It was going on midnight, and I sure wasn't going to be able to get me a cab due to the fact that all of the cabs were driving the drunk people home from the bar. This was kind of different because they were driving a drunk guy away from home this time.

I got a hold of the cab dispatcher on the phone, gave them my address, and asked how much it would cost to get me to where I needed to go. They estimated me at twenty dollars there and back, so I was looking at a forty-dollar trip. I came up with the smart idea of trying to save money on the way back and just have the cabdriver drop me off at Swamp's on the way back because he was closer. The next twenty minutes felt like they took forever to pass by as I waited for the cabdriver to show up. I kept thinking to myself that this cabdriver was going to mess up the whole night and I would end up like my roommate, passed out with nothing.

Out of the darkness of the night, I saw the bright lights of the cab coming creeping up to my house. It almost looked like one of those slow pass-bys that gangsters make before they shoot up a place. You know just so they know that they have the right address. After all, who wanted to shoot up the wrong person? That just ruins all of the plans. The cab stopped, and I made my way over to the cab. The driver rolled down my window and asked if I were the one who called the dispatcher. I mean, was that even really a question he should have asked? I'm pretty positive that, if I weren't the person who called, I wouldn't have walked over to the cab in the first place.

I answered the cabdriver's question and hopped on in. The cabdriver asked where I was heading to, and I still didn't have the address of my destination. I had to call Siren back to tell her I was on my way. I told the cabdriver to start heading over to Lynnwood, the next town over from me in Oregon. I dialed Siren's number, and once again after a few short rings, she picked up, and the voiceover took me once again. I told Siren I was on my way and said I needed to know where her address was. As Siren told me the number, I repeated them aloud to the cabdriver so he could put them into his GPS.

The next thing I heard on the phone was the voice of worry, and I thought for sure it was about to blow all of my plans for the night. Siren started to question me if I were a cop and whom I was talking to. I'm not going to lie. I should have thought it through more, and I sure wasn't about ready to tell her I was drunk. So I made up a quick lie. I told Siren that my license had been revoked because I got into a pretty bad car accident not too long ago and I was having a cabdriver taking me to her place. The funny part was that I did get into a car accident during the winter because of the icy roads, but it was never reported.

Siren finally calmed down and started to trust me again. It wasn't like I had anything to hide from her. I wasn't a part of any law enforcement, and if I were, I was sure that I wouldn't have blown it over the phone. I told Siren I would be there as quickly as I could and I would call her when I got closer to her place. I hung up the phone and asked the cabdriver if he got the address

I had given him. The cabdriver told me that I would be there in five minutes. Yeah, that was what we thought until we got lost.

Siren had given me the right address. The only problem was that she gave me the address to the apartment complex she lived in, and the cabdriver drove right past it the first time. We both thought that we were looking for a house, which was not the case at all. The cabdriver eventually made a turn around and headed back the other way. This time, he managed to drive us another few miles out of the opposite way this time. Since I was in the area, I thought this would be a good time to call Siren and get the facts straight on where I was supposed to be at. I dialed Siren's number yet again, and after a few short rings, she picked up.

I explained to Siren that I was having a hard time trying to find her house and I could not locate the address. Siren told me that she forgot to explain about the fact that she lived in an apartment. That would have been nice to know from the beginning. Now the problem was trying to figure out which apartment complex was hers. Over in Lynnwood by the mall area, there happens to be several apartment complexes, and yes, some of them look exactly alike.

The cabdriver then turned around and asked if he could talk to Siren. Now since I was drunk, it seemed like a good idea at the time. Now, I look back and laugh and wonder if the cabdriver really knew whom I was talking to and if he knew what I was going to be doing that night. I mean, how many people let their random cabdrivers talk to their prostitutes?

The cabdriver stayed on the phone with Siren the whole time until he pulled up to the front of the apartment complex. He stopped the cab at the very first apartment and told me that I was going to have to walk to her place. I guess this would make sense. She was trying to keep everything quiet, and she didn't want the whole world exposed to what she did for a living.

Before I got back on the phone with Siren, I asked the cabdriver for his number so I could secure a ride over to Swamp's place. The cabdriver gave me his business card. I got out of the cab and closed the door, and we both went on our way.

I turned my attention to being back on the phone with Siren and started asking her where her apartment was. I was sure that, if I could go back in time and see me running around this apartment complex looking for this place, I would die of laughter. Siren kept trying to lead me to her front door the best she could without having to come outside. I figured, if it were just me, she could have come and got me. It wasn't like I had a recording crew with me to catch her on camera.

I must have ran around that apartment complex for a half hour before I finally got to her front door. It always seemed like she would have me run past her door in one direction or another. Who knows? Maybe she was watching me to make sure no one was following me.

I finally arrived at Siren's front door, and as soon as I got there, I didn't even have a chance to knock before she opened the door. She was exactly how she looked in the pictures. The only thing was that she was a lot shorter than how she looked in the pictures. Siren stood only five-foot-three when she looked at least five inches taller in the pictures. It just goes to show you can make camera angles work for you.

Siren looked at me with the biggest smile on her face and asked me to come in. She warned me about her dog that was locked up in the bathroom and asked if I had an allergies. I wasn't sure why she would have asked me this thing now and not earlier on the phone, but it didn't matter either way. Siren walked me into the living room area and had me sit down on this elegant white couch she had. This apartment was just how you would have imagined it to be. Everything had its very own spot, and nothing looked like it was out of order. I was afraid to touch anything and have the wrath of God come down upon through the form of a prostitute.

Siren sat down in the recliner that was adjacent to the couch, and she put me through a small interview process. I knew what she was looking for, but I'm not going to reveal what she was looking for in this book because I believe in the working woman. She asked the pretty basic questions about what I did and where I was from. Siren then filled me in about her life and why she was doing what she doing. She was a college student living on her own, trying to pay for all of her bills and her tuition. She was a double major and double minor trying to get into the medical field. Siren then stated that she had to make $2,000 just to pay her bills and tuition and live. Talk about an expensive life.

The interview process ended. We both stood up and started to strip each other down. This is a big part of being with a prostitute. The way you both get completely naked can tell you a lot of signs about the other person. I wish I could say it was easy, but there really is a science to it, and if you don't pay attention to the signs, you could be the one getting screwed. Once the both of us were completely naked, Siren led me to the bedroom. This bedroom was set up differently because all it had was a bed in it and nothing else.

I couldn't help but ask Siren why there was only a bed in the room. This was the room she specifically took all of her clients into. The thought of how many people have had sex in a person's bed never really crossed my mind, but this bed did. If you have a bed that is set aside for people just to have sex in, I'm sure that hundreds of people have had sex in that bed and I would be rolling around in all of it. I guess this thought should have bothered me, but when I was a teenager, both my brother and my sister had sex with other people in my bed. For what reason I don't know why, they didn't like to tell me things like that until a few days later. It's kind of a fucked-up thing to do to a person.

Siren had me lay down on the bed facedown, and I instantly sunk right in. I never had sex on a memory foam mattress or even laid on one, but I knew I wasn't going to want to get off this bed. Siren climbed on the bed right after I did, and she proceeded to give me a back massage. I've never had this happen to me in the States before where I got a massage before sex, but I could start getting used to this. The massage only lasted about five minutes before Siren wanted to get down to business, and

I wasn't complaining. I rolled over as Siren got off the bed for a quick second to get a condom out of her pocket. Once again, someone was looking out for our best interests.

Siren climbed back on the bed, ripped the condom wrapper open, and took it out. It started off the exact same way, a quick pre–blow job to get me started, and then Siren put the condom on. Remember when I told you that all of the drinking I did earlier would work for me and against me? Well, that was what happened.

My dick stayed hard forever, and we went through every position we could think of twice. We started in missionary, doggie, cowgirl, reverse cowgirl, and repeat. At one point, I even picked her up, got off the bed, and fucked her standing. The only problem I was having was that I was so drunk that I wasn't cumming at all. I wasn't even close to cumming, and this was getting bad.

Sure, it's everyone's fantasy to have sex last forever, but it really takes its toll on you. You get tired and want to sleep. Random pains start setting in, and emotions get in the way because you are getting too pissed at the fact that an end doesn't seem close in sight. I never wanted or want to do this again during sex, but I actually had to have Siren stop having sex with me and give me a hand job because I was so fucking tired.

Siren couldn't even believe what I was saying. She proceeded to laugh as she asked me if I took a Viagra before I came over. I couldn't help but laugh because of the prior experience I had with Viagra, but I was so glad I didn't take one tonight.

Siren took off the condom and stood over me with her ass facing me and her head facing the other way. She bent over and started giving me a hand job as I started feeling her ass. After a few minutes, I decided I would move away from her ass and start to finger her. That was when she stopped me. Do you believe this? I actually got stopped for trying to return the favor. Siren told me that she didn't know where my hands had been and she didn't want to get her vagina dirty. Okay, this made sense, but at the same time, it seemed a little far-fetched. My dick was just inside of her, and she was worried about my fingers. How the fuck did that make sense?

That was the first time I got stopped. The second time I got stopped, once again, I got tired of lying there and wanted to get involved with doing something. I sat up a little bit and tried to grab her tits. I got stopped this time because Siren had boob implants done a few weeks ago and didn't know if they were completely healed yet. Honestly for having fake boobs, I couldn't even tell by looking at them or feeling what I did to them. I do have to say so myself that fake boobs are pretty cool in my book, but I would say only get them if you truly feel you need them. All woman are beautiful, and you shouldn't have to change your looks to get what you want. But you should do it if you truly feel that it will make you happy. Everyone deserves happiness.

For the remaining time I spent at Siren's apartment, all I did was lay there and let her finish the job. The end still seemed like it took forever because I was still trying to wear off some of the booze from earlier. Finally when the end seemed like it was never going to happen, I just let it come out. I never gave Siren any warning, and I just shot my load. Some of my cum landed in her hair, but most of it was either on the bed or myself. I hate ending sex with a hand job, but this was one of those occasions where it needed to happen. This long sexual journey ended just in time because I drifted off into a sleep right after.

I wasn't out for long, probably about fifteen minutes at most. Siren woke me up, and there she was, standing on the side of the bed in a bathrobe, trying to hand me a wet nap so I could clean up the cum that landed on me. I took the wet nap, cleaned everything up, and lay on the bed for another few seconds. Siren wanted me out of her apartment, and I could tell. She was handing me my clothes and telling me that I needed to call my ride. Siren went from being cool to being a bitch in a few seconds flat. It wasn't like I planned on moving in. I was just trying to recollect myself so I could leave. So I got started on getting out. I put on my clothes as fast as I could and called the cabdriver from earlier.

I told the cabdriver to meet me out at the front to the apartment complex where he dropped me off. As soon as I hung up the phone, Siren forced me out the door. Can you believe that I didn't even get a kiss good-bye? What a shame.

I walked from Siren's apartment to the front of the complex just to wait for the cabdriver. It only took him about ten minutes to show up this time, and luckily for me, he didn't drive past this time. The cabdriver never asked me what exactly happened that night, but I believe he knew that something happened. I stuck to my plan and had the cabdriver drop me off at Swamp's place. I knew it was the early hours in the morning. It must have been around two in the morning, to be exact, but Swamp said I was always welcome over at any time. So I figured I would take him up on that.

I got to Swamp's door, and I was going to find out if he were awake or not. I knocked and waited for a few minutes, but Swamp finally answered the door. It turned out he was awake the whole time and Spark was even at his place hanging out that night. I sat down for a second and talked with Swamp and Spark about what I just did before the sleepiness overtook me. I fell asleep on the floor, and that was all I remembered from the night. It was a good thing it was the weekend because I sure didn't want to go to work the next day.

The weekend passed, and it was back to work. Early that morning, my supervisor handed me a stack of papers and told me that he wanted to update everyone's emergency contact information. We had picked up some new people along the way, and some people even moved living spaces so it was only fair. I made it through the whole list and got down to the newest supervisor that we just got. Since he wasn't in the system before, I had to get everything from the beginning from his name, his spouse's name, his phone number, and his address. Once I had all of the information, I told him thank you, and he went on his way.

Something about his address kept bothering me because it looked so familiar, but I could not think of where I saw it. I asked both Ops and Swamp what their addresses were, and they didn't match up. I kept thinking to myself that I'd been here before, but I'd never been over to his house. And I didn't know anyone who lived there.

I spent most of the day trying to think about where I knew his address from. I ran through my phone and checked all of my text messages, and that even came up to a dead end. It wasn't until I got home that night that it finally clicked in my head. The prostitute I just had sex with lived in the same complex as my boss.

I couldn't help but think if I should be worried or laugh about the whole situation. I mean, after all, everyone knew I did it, and it would have been funny if that were the first impression he had on me. On the other hand, I could have been right across the hall from him, and this whole time, he was living next to a prostitute. Imagine what the cops would have done if they ever busted her. I sure hope he figured out who his neighbors really were.

I can't really say that I had a deep-down moral connection with this story, but I did learn something I'll carry with me for the rest of my life. Try not to drink too much before you have sex because you might get more than what you bargained for. Try to find out where your bosses live so you can avoid running into someone you know, especially if you are screwing a prostitute because that would be an awkward situation for everyone. The last thing, buy a memory foam mattress for a great night of sleep and sex.

THE LAST ONE

If the title of this chapter didn't give it away, this was the last prostitute I have slept with to date. There were more in between all of these stories, but not all of them were that exciting. Most of the stories, it was the usual makeup. After the phone call, I either traveled over to her place, or she came to me. I paid her the money, we had sex, and on her way she went. Throughout my entire time sleeping with prostitutes, I kept count and ended at thirty even. Not bad, if I say so myself. I know that some people out there have slept with more than I have and probably have been sleeping with prostitutes for years. The only difference between those people and me is that I'm willing to tell everyone about it.

I was still in Oregon at this time, but I would be leaving soon. I got the news around November 2011 that I would be losing my job and there wasn't much I could do about it. Here I was knowing that everything I knew up until this moment was coming to an end. It wasn't the greatest experience of my life, but I made it though, and life is good again. I wasn't really going to work much these days because I was having to get my stuff ready to move back home so my boss would usually either let me go early or tell me not to come in that day. I'll have to admit that moving back home after being on your own sucks.

One of the days my boss gave me off, I figured I would make the best of it and spend it by saying good-bye to everyone I met along the way. So I made my stops at all of the stripper coffee stands I used to go to every day, and I even stopped by the local porn store and said good-bye to the manager who I had become friends with over the year. Reality was starting to set in, and it was getting worse by the day. I'm not going to lie. I really loved my job. I got to travel all around the world. I made some good money and got to know some really cool people, and I lived on the other side of the country away from my family. It was like a dream come true.

After I said all of my good-byes, I made my way back home to find myself overtaken by boredom. I needed to do something to cheer me up and take my mind off all the stress. I figured I would give it one last good run and see what I could find online. I started looking through all of the ads, and I came across the same one several times. I thought to myself, "Either this girl is trying to get her name out there and make some money, or this is a setup." That would have been pretty funny to get arrested after losing my job for sleeping with a prostitute. Talk about going out with a bang.

The girl in the ad stood about five-foot-nothing with highlighted hair down to her ass. She was a little bit of a thicker girl, but she had an ass most guys would die to get with. I said, "What the hell?" and called the number.

A few short rings went by, and the girl from the ad picked up the phone. It was the same standard conversation. I asked if she were real, she asked where I was located, and then I asked how much it would cost. You get so used to doing it after a while that you start to think it's something that happens on the daily in everyone's life. You forget that you are breaking the law after a while, and you even forget what the purpose of having a real relationship is like. For safety measures of this story, I'm going to call her Last because she was the last one.

Last quoted me at $200 and told me that she would be coming from Tacoma, which was about an hour south of where I was. This worked out because I still had to run to an ATM. I told her to call me back when she got close and I would tell her how to get to my place.

I hung up the phone and made a quick trip to the ATM to get my money. I know I probably shouldn't have spent the money I had left on a prostitute, especially since I was losing my job, which meant I was losing my paycheck, but you only get one life.

I got back to my place and sat around waiting for almost two hours. I thought this was getting kind of strange because she should have been here by now. I decided to call Last back and see if she were still available. The phone rang, but there was no answer, so I tried again. There was no answer the second time, and I thought to myself that she wasn't coming. In all honesty, if she didn't show up, it wouldn't have bothered me. I probably didn't need to spend the money anyway.

I continued with my day and packed up some more of my stuff. Not too long, I felt that taking a nap would be a good idea, and I fell asleep. My phone ringing about three hours later woke me up. I answered the phone, and Last was on the other end. She explained how she made a stop by her friend's house and how they ran out to get something. I'm not sure what "something" was, but I have a good idea. She said that, when she left her friend's house, she accidentally left her phone inside the house and couldn't return my phone call until just now. I explained to Last that I fell asleep anyway so I wasn't too worried about it. It then came down to the question of if I were still interested.

I already had out the money, my roommate was home, and I really wasn't doing anything. So I figured that I would have her stop on by. I wish I would have thought about saying yes because, when she showed up, she wasn't in the best condition. She wasn't bad, but you could tell that she had been doing something. Last's car pulled up about an hour after I got off the phone with her, and I could tell something was wrong by the way she parked. Last tried to parallel park her car, but half of her car was sticking out in the street. I knew this was going to be a fun time.

Last got out of the car, and by the looks of her, the ad didn't lie. She was a little short thing with a nice, big, fat ass. I swear most of her body weight was in her ass. I met her outside and introduced myself. It's not like anyone else was going to say hi to her first, but I figured I would be nice and walk her to my door. When I got next to her, I noticed that she had an unreasonable amount of perfume on, and I felt I just had to say something. She told me that she had a few shots of whiskey and smoked a joint before she came over. I don't know if this were good customer service or if I should have been worried about her getting a DUI. Bad decision and negative morals just filled this whole situation.

I led Last into my house and straight to my bedroom. If you recall from earlier, I explained how posters of porn stars and other half-naked women covered my room. As soon as Last stepped into my room, all of the posters hanging up instantly mesmerized her, and she didn't move, almost as if she were stuck in a trance. I let her look around the room for a few minutes before I finally asked her if everything were all right. The one thing I didn't need right now was a prostitute running out of my place screaming because she felt uncomfortable with her surroundings.

Last snapped out of her trance and came back to. I asked her again if anything were wrong. All the posters

I had so intrigued her that she never wanted to leave my room. Just then all of the questions started. She asked where I got the posters, if I were a collector, how much porn I watched, and if I slept with prostitutes on a regular basis. I answered every question as truthfully as I could without making everything seem too obvious. Last must have had a short attention span or the alcohol and weed were kicking in pretty good because, every time I went to say something, her attention went back over to my posters.

I figured I wouldn't waste any more time and just get to it before Last's attention got stuck forever on my posters, leaving my empty-handed. I asked Last if she were ready to get started, and she came back to with a smile on her face. She asked me for the money and said to put it on the counter so she knew I had it. After this, we both started taking off our clothes, making sure that we were both ready to go through with this. There wasn't turning back now, so without any hesitation, I got my clothes off as quickly as I could and helped Last with the rest of what she had on.

In no time, I had Last on the bed, and I was ready to go. Last stopped me and said she wanted to get the condoms she had out of her purse. Last jumped off my bed for a quick second, grabbed her purse, and got out the condom, and we were in good business.

Last took the condom out of the wrapper, and I laid there and waited for her to put it on. I had done this multiple times before, but this time was starting to feel different. While knowing this would be the last prostitute I slept with for a while or ever again, the thought of trying to enjoy this to the fullest started to flow through my head. I couldn't believe this was coming to an end. Everything I had done over the past few years was all ending like this. I thought back to all of the prostitutes I slept with along the way and started thinking of all the good times I had along the way. During the whole time I spent thinking about this, Last already had the condom and was done with the warm-up blow job. Last was talking to me, trying to get my attention, and I came back to reality.

I stopped letting all of the thoughts of past prostitutes get to me as I looked Last in the eyes, grabbed her, and rolled us both over as I got on top of her. With Last laying on the bed, I didn't waste any time getting right to it. The sex positions never changed during this interaction. Last was so sucked into my posters that I just let her do whatever. It was pretty boring. Think of it as the couple who only has sex on a regular basis but aren't quite sure what they are doing or if they are really interested in each other. Yeah, I was kind of like that.

I blew my load and got off Last, and the sex was finally over. It was a sad way to go out, I'll have to admit, but you can't always get what you want in life. I sat on the edge of my bed with all of the thoughts still pouring through my head. I stared at the floor for a while before Last asked me if everything were fine.

I lied to Last and said, "Yeah, everything is good."

I had no choice. I couldn't fill her in on three years of prostitutes in a short amount of time. Besides, I was sure she wouldn't want to hear about it anyway. Last told me that I used the only condom she had in her purse and she was going to have to pick up more. I told her not to worry about it. I said I would hook her up.

I walked into my closet and grabbed the cardboard box I used to keep full of condoms. The box must have been a quarter full, but I didn't really have a use for it anymore. I sure wasn't going to fly it home with me.

I handed Last the box and told her, "Merry Christmas."

Last stood in shock and told her I probably saved her at least a few hundred dollars, creating more of a profit for her in the short term. I honestly couldn't think of a better present to give a prostitute besides straight cash.

Last and I put our clothes back on and looked around to make sure she wasn't forgetting anything. Last grabbed the money off the counter, and as she tried to put it into her purse, a bag of weed fell out. So now she had drugs on her. She was on drugs and drunk. It goes to show that this woman gave no fucks. Last picked up the weed, apologized, and then asked me if I wanted to smoke. I politely refused. I never really was interested in smoking or doing drugs, but I've been known to throw that moral out the window when I get really drunk like once or maybe twice a year.

I walked Last out of her car and said my good-byes to her. I knew I shouldn't have let her drive under the condition she was in, but it wasn't really my place to tell her how to live. After all, we were both making decisions most normal people wouldn't.

Last got in her car, shut the door, and drove away. It was just a matter of time for her to go from being the prostitute I just slept with to being another memory in my life. I turned away from the street and headed back into my place, only to start packing again.

Most of the posters and porn I owned were thrown away. The one poster I managed to save was the Tera Patrick poster I had ever since I was sixteen. I couldn't ever throw that away. I threw away a few thousand dollars I invested into my life as I closed the chapter on my crazy sexual adventure.

The only thing I can say about this experience is that, in life, all good things come to an end. Even if that good thing is for a good or bad reason, everything ends at some point. Now I fit in with the rest of everyone and live a normal life. I haven't slept with a prostitute in more than three years. I do the typical things now and go out to the bar, trying to find normal woman to sleep with, spending money on drinks, and sometimes not getting anywhere. Talk about having a boring life.

Epilogue

I hope that, with my insight and my crazy stories, everyone who reads this can find some type of positive lesson he or she has learned. As I've stated many times in this book, prostitutes aren't bad people. They're just like me and you, blending into society and trying to do what they can to get by. You have to put yourself into their shoes and think about it. If you back into a corner and are down on your luck, I'm sure you are going to do anything you can to survive.

I do believe that prostitution should be legalized, but it should be regulated as well. By putting restrictions on it, we can create guidelines to protect the interests of both parties. Everyone likes having sex. Why not make it easy for everyone to have it? We're all sexual beings in the world, and by having sex, we are just completing the roles we were meant to carry out. The amount of people who don't have sex regularly is just a sign that we are not fulfilling an essential part of life.

The fact that some people aren't having sex sometimes has nothing to do with the person at all—but rather what others think of that person. We've become a society that bases all of our opinions on what the media tells us. If most of us don't look like celebrities or models, most people won't take the time to even look at us. Everyone wants to fit in with the in crowd, yet all forget about those who helped them along the way.

I'm sure everyone who reads this book can probably think of the first person he or she had sex with, and now that person has become nothing more than just a person you fucked back in the day. You got what you wanted out of that person and threw him or her to side, only to move onto the next. Even something as simple as sex can leave a lasting impression on someone. So by legalizing prostitution, all you are really doing is helping the people who get rejected link up with those who are willing to fulfill their sexual desires.

As for me, I lost my job, moved back home, and started hanging out with my old crowd again. It wasn't the plan I had for my life, but things happen. I dated Love for a while, but even that ended. One day, she decided she wanted to be with someone else over me, and I took it pretty hard. I couldn't tell you why I decided to stop sleeping with prostitutes, but I'm sure it could be for a number of reasons. Maybe I grew out of it and figured it was time to move on in life. Maybe I couldn't afford it anymore, or possibly I finally decided that I wanted to have a relationship with someone.

I usually go around telling my stories to people, as they all get a laugh out of them and ask me questions of why I did all of it. That inspired me to write this book. I figured I would share them with the world and let people into my life. I did get tested when I got home, and I can say that I am completely clean. I guess it was just the luck of the draw. I couldn't be happier that I didn't catch anything, and I am grateful for that every day. Most of the time now, before I sleep with anyone, I tell her straight to her face about how I used to sleep with prostitutes because I feel that it's only fair.

Every now and then, I still look at all of the ads online just to see what's out there if I ever do decide to give it another try in my life. I guess, after all, you never really forget about the past, and you never know when it will come back into your life. What can I say? They had me hooked.

About the Author

I was born and raised just outside of Detroit, Michigan. Ever since childhood, I always dreamed of traveling the world and seeing just how the other side lives. From my late teen years into my early twenties, I left home and spent some time traveling and visiting everywhere from Japan to Russia and the rest of the world. My goal for writing is to tell people about my stories and travels over the years to help inspire others to live their lives to the fullest and share their stories as well. You only get one chance. You might as well make the best of it.